GW01368351

ISBN 978-1-333-96207-4
PIBN 10697582

FB &c Ltd, Dalton House, 60 Windsor Avenue, London, SW19 2RR.
Company number 08720141. Registered in England and Wales.

For support please visit www.forgottenbooks.com

Book One

The Sunday-School Teacher's Bible

Published October, 1907

From the Society's own Press

GENERAL NOTE

The National Teacher-training Institute is a department of the American Baptist Publication Society. For years this Society has, through its State Sunday-school missionaries conducted teacher-training work, each missionary doing the work after his own heart. The awakening of the country to the crying need of religious education, and of the church to the fact that the Sunday-school is first and foremost in the winning of the world to Christ, calls for a uniform and up-to-date system of teacher training. This system the Society now offers to the public in the work of its National Teacher-training Institute.

Training for Sunday-school work, like all other training, should proceed upon correct educational principles and methods. Educational principles and methods are determined by human nature and historic needs. The National Teacher-training text-books are prepared from these points of view. These books are as follows: "The Sunday-school Teacher's Bible"; "The Sunday-school Teacher's Pupils"; "The Sunday-school Teacher's Pedagogy"; "The Sunday-school Teacher's School"; and "Teaching Missions in the Sunday-school." The aim of these books is to furnish the teachers and officers of our Sunday-schools with a working knowledge of the Bible as a book and as the message of God to men, of the personality of the pupils with whom they have to deal, of the principles and methods of pedagogy as applied to Sunday-school teaching, of the organization, aim, and work of the Sunday-school as a school, and of the best ways and means of introducing and conducting mission study in the Sunday-school. The books thus cover every phase of Sunday-school service.

SUGGESTIONS TO TEACHERS AND STUDENTS

1. Note that our teacher-training text-books are not built up with the idea that teacher training is a process of memorizing facts and figures by means of diagrams manufactured to order. Our aim has been to stimulate thought and arouse the will to action. Facts are given but these are to be acquired by using the seeing and doing faculties of the soul as well as photographing. "Learning by memory only is the besetting of learning." In learning by thinking and doing we not only increase our knowledge but develop our personalities. This aim underlies all our teacher-training work.

2. Note that our teacher-training system is built up by units of study. Each study is complete in itself, and finds its basis in one of our text-books as a rule. Most of these studies consist of twenty lessons. Some, however, contain thirty, and a few forty. It will be seen that the work is thus specific, each study forming a definite piece of work. This is the conception of education in our best colleges and universities to-day. When one unit of study has been completed the class or correspondent pupil can go on to others "as they like it."

3. The teacher of the training class is left free in the conduct of the teaching work, making his own illustrations, etc., according to his own ideas and the need of the class in hand. In suggesting "Topics for Class Discussion" we call attention to a fundamental factor in all true education —that of expression on the part of the pupil. The lecture

method, as a rule, is out of place in the Sunday-school training. Let the class take part in the lesson work. The "Topics for Class Papers" call for some real learning by doing—some research work on the part of the pupil. Nothing will bring better results in the work than this.

4. The teacher-training class, to do the best work, should have a class library. Out of the reference literature suggested a dozen books could be selected without great cost. Correspondence pupils will be able also to do better work if they can purchase two or three books of reference to be used in connection with these studies. Wherever desired the editor of our own text-books will suggest the books for the class library, and also for the correspondence pupil. In regard to the reference literature in general, we have given books which present different views of questions as yet unsettled. The student is thus able to learn his subject from all points of view. The wider the range of knowledge on the part of the teacher to-day the greater will be his efficiency for service. Of course each person is free to use the books of reference he wishes and to form his own conclusions.

H. T. M.

SEPTEMBER 1, 1907.

CONTENTS

PART I

A GENERAL INTRODUCTION TO THE BIBLE

PART II

THE GREAT VITAL DOCTRINES OF THE BIBLE

Part I

A General Introduction to the Bible

"Study to show thyself approved unto God, a workman that needeth not to be ashamed, rightly dividing the word of truth."—2 Tim. 2 : 5.

LESSON I

THE BIBLE AS A BOOK AND AS LITERATURE

Reference literature. Hamill, "The Books of the Bible"; Moulton, "A Short Introduction to the Literature of the Bible"; Smyth, "How We Got Our Bible"; Kent, "The Origin and Permanent Value of the Old Testament."

1. *The Bible as a book.* What is the Bible? First of all it is a book. There it is in your hands, just a book. That is the first thing we learn about the Bible. Many people never get any farther in their knowledge of it. To them it is always just a book. To the Sunday-school teacher it must become the Book of all books.

2. *The Bible as a book of two parts.* If we wish to go a step farther in our knowledge of the Bible we must open it. On doing this we find it is a book of two parts. Part I is called "The Old Testament"; Part II, "The New Testament." What is the meaning of the word "testament" and of the words "old" and "new" as used with it? The word "testament" as applied to the Bible really means "covenant." Covenant in the biblical sense means, not a compact between two parties, but "an irrevocable promise made by God to his people, freely and on his absolute authority, a promise of a religious inheritance into which they could enter by fulfilling the conditions which God, on the same absolute authority, imposed." (Ramsay.) The conditions imposed are, however, a part of his beneficent arrangement. Paul's thought is that the covenant is the outgrowth of God's free grace. Hence, in translating the Bible from the Greek into Latin

the word *testamentum* (the imposed will or covenant of a superior) was used rather than *fœdus* (a covenant between equals). Thus *testamentum* came to be the classic title of the documents containing the attested promises of blessing willed by God and bequeathed to man in the death of Christ. The "Old" Testament means, therefore, God's gracious covenant with his chosen people that he would bless them and make them a blessing. The "New" Testament means God's final and full covenant with man of salvation through Jesus Christ. This covenant has been sealed by the death of his Son.

3. *The Bible as a book of many books.* Looking more closely at the Bible we find that it is a book made up of many books. It is a library in itself—"a divine library," as Jerome called it. There are sixty-six books in all—thirty-nine in the Old Testament and twenty-seven in the New. It is from this fact that the Bible gets its name. The name "The Bible" is really in the plural. It came from *ta biblia,* which means "the books." Biblia came from *biblos,* the name of a papyrus reed out of whose fibers the leaves of ancient books were made. (Our word paper is derived from papyrus.) *Ta biblia,* the Greek plural, came to be used as a Latin singular, and so we get the name "The Bible," which means "The Book." In the early days of the church the term *ta biblia* was applied sometimes to the books of the Old Testament alone and sometimes to all the books of the Bible.

With reference to the character and purpose of their writing the books of the Bible may be arranged somewhat logically as on the following page. It will be well for each pupil to commit these tables to memory as a rule, though the class should not waste time on mere drilling. In this arrangement the time element does not enter. In Lessons V and VI an effort is made to give the different books their historical setting.

I. THE OLD TESTAMENT.

Legal Books.	*Historical Books.*	*Poetical Books.*	*Prophetical Books.*
1. Genesis.	1. Joshua.	1. Job.	1. Isaiah.
2. Exodus.	2. Judges.	2. Psalms.	2. Jeremiah.
3. Leviticus.	3. Ruth.	3. Proverbs.	3. Ezekiel.
4. Numbers.	4. 1 Samuel.	4. Ecclesiastes.	4. Daniel.
5. Deuteronomy.	5. 2 Samuel.	5. Song of Solomon.	5. Hosea.
	6. 1 Kings.	6. Lamentations.	6. Joel.
	7. 2 Kings.		7. Amos.
	8. 1 Chronicles.		8. Obadiah.
	9. 2 Chronicles.		9. Jonah.
	10. Ezra.		10. Micah.
	11. Nehemiah.		11. Nahum.
	12. Esther.		12. Habakkuk.
			13. Zephaniah.
			14. Haggai.
			15. Zechariah.
			16. Malachi.

II. THE NEW TESTAMENT.

Historical Books.	*Pauline Epistles.*	*General Epistles and Revelation.*
1. Matthew.	1. Romans.	1. James.
2. Mark.	2. 1 Corinthians.	2. 1 Peter.
3. Luke.	3. 2 Corinthians.	3. 2 Peter.
4. John.	4. Galatians.	4. 1 John.
5. Acts.	5. Ephesians.	5. 2 John.
	6. Philippians.	6. 3 John.
	7. Colossians.	7. Jude.
	8. 1 Thessalonians.	8. Hebrews.
	9. 2 Thessalonians.	9. Revelation.
	10. 1 Timothy.	
	11. 2 Timothy.	
	12. Titus.	
	13. Philemon.	

These sixty-six books constitute what is called the *canon* of the Scriptures. The word "canon," which originally meant a straight line or rule, was used to denote the list of books whereby the contents of the Scriptures could be correctly defined. All other writings were considered apocryphal. In the formation of the canon every book of the Bible was subjected to rigorous tests, "those that stood the test of time and scholarship and experience making the canon." The canon of the Old Testament was largely determined by Ezra, the Great Synagogue, and Nehemiah. As nearly all the books of the Old Testament are quoted in the New Testament, the Old Testament canon must have been fully established by the time of Christ. The canon of the New Testament was gradually fixed by the growing agreement of the Christian churches, and was authoritatively settled by the Council of Carthage A. D. 397.

4. *The Bible as a book of literature.* The Bible is a book of literature. "No doubt the word literary is used in many different senses; what I have in mind is the various forms of which a literature is made up. When we speak of Greek literature or English literature every one thinks of certain dramas, epics, philosophical works, histories, poems, stories, and the like, produced by the Greek or English peoples. If then the Bible is to be called literature, we ought to expect to find in it dramas, stories, philosophical works, histories, songs, and similar forms of literature" (Moulton). All these are found in it, and in sublimity of thought and beauty of expression are second to none in the world of literature. No book has influenced the literature of modern nations so much as the Bible. Justin Martyr claimed that the best in the ancient literature of the Greeks and Romans was gotten from Moses and the prophets of the Old Testament.

We may classify the literature of the Bible in several ways. Perhaps as good a way as any is as follows: First, *legal literature*. This literature is made up of statutes, precepts, judgments, laws. These are usually given with their historical setting or deliverance. Thus even the law, save in few places, is full of freshness to the student. A large part of the books of Exodus, Leviticus, Numbers, and Deuteronomy belong to this form of literature. Deuteronomy is a great series of sermons on the law and its blessings and cursings according as it is obeyed or disobeyed. Secondly, there is the *historical literature*. Much history is found in the Pentateuch, or the legal books. But this literature is found chiefly in the books of the Old Testament from Joshua to Esther. Some of these books were written by prophets and some by priests. From a literary point of view the prophets are more vigorous than the priests. In certain parts of this history the narrative is a model of literary style; in others it takes the form of the chronicle. The book of Acts in the New Testament belongs also to the historical literature. Thirdly, the *prophetical literature.* In the historical books some of the sayings of the early prophets are preserved. How early these prophets began to preach we do not know. By the eighth century B. C. they began to put their predictions and sermons in literary form. There are seventeen of these "writing" prophets in all—Isaiah to Malachi. This literature is chiefly sermonic in form. These prophets were great preachers of righteousness in their day. Fourthly, the *wisdom literature.* The Jews as a people were not given to philosophy. Their wisdom sayings, as a rule, grow out of their experiences and hopes. The wisdom literature consists of the books of Job, Proverbs, Ecclesiastes, and the Song of Solomon. Some of the most beautiful things in the world of human thought are found in these books. Fifthly, there is a book of *devotional literature* in the Bible—the book of Psalms. It is the prayer-book and hymn-book of the people of Israel. The sweep of religious experience in this is world wide and humanity deep. In it is found somewhere a sample of nearly every experience common to the devotional life of man. Besides the book of Psalms passages of devotional literature are found in other books of the Bible. Sixthly, *biographical literature.* The Bible is full of great men, and here and there in it their lives are briefly sketched. There is, however, one preeminent person in the Bible—Jesus the Christ. Parts of the Old Testament are devoted to prophecies of his coming. Four books of the New Testament are devoted exclusively to his life and teachings, and these are not too many. No other life is so essential to the moral and religious welfare of this world. Each biographer writes of him from a different angle of vision. Matthew looks upon him as the promised Messiah; Mark sees him as the mighty worker of beneficent deeds; Luke finds in him the friend and Saviour of all mankind; and John beholds him as the divine Son of God—the Word made flesh. Seventhly, the *epistolary literature.* A large part of the New Testament is made up of letters. There are the letters of Paul—thirteen in number. Two letters are ascribed to Peter, and three to John. One is ascribed to Jude. Last of all the letter to the Hebrews by an unknown author. These letters are devoted to the doctrinal and practical aspects of Christianity in the early days of the church. Through them God has given a message for all time. The book of Revelation is often classified with prophetic literature, though it properly belongs with apocalypse—a form of writing current in Palestine after the decline of prophecy.

Topics for Class Discussion

1. The meaning of the word "testament."
2. The books of the Bible as to their classification.
3. The Bible as a book of literature.
4. The poetry of the Bible.
5. Favorite selections from the literature of the Bible.

Topics for Class Papers

1. The Bible as a book of many books.
2. The literary study of the Bible.

LESSON II

THE DIVINE ORIGIN OF THE BIBLE

Alvah Hovey, D. D., LL. D.

Reference literature. Hovey, "The Bible"; Dods, "The Bible, Its Origin and Nature"; Geistweit, "The Young Christian and His Bible"; Manly, "The Bible Doctrine of Inspiration"; Sanday, "The Oracles of God"; Torrey, "The Divine Origin of the Bible."

1. *The Bible is from God.* To explain and verify this proposition will be the object of this chapter. This proposition does not mean that every sentence of the Bible expresses a thought of God; for a large part of the volume preserves the thoughts of men who were not inspired, perhaps not renewed, while a considerable part of it preserves the sentiments of evil men or of malignant spirits. Nor does it mean that God by his Spirit dictated to these sacred writers the very words which in all cases they used, so that children might have been employed as naturally as men in giving the Bible its actual form; for to this theory there are grave objections. But the proposition means that in some way God enabled the sacred writers to put on record just what he wished them, acting in his name, to say to men. And surely he wished them to give truth, not falsehood, to mankind. Hence by saying that the Bible is from God it is affirmed that all its language, rightly interpreted, is strictly true and divinely important.

2. *The first evidence of its divine origin.* To verify this proposition, as now explained, it may be well to notice, in the first place, the accuracy of the Bible in statements not strictly religious. In doing this one naturally begins with the New Testament, for Christianity, as a historical

religion, took its rise in Palestine about thirty years after the Christian era, and before the close of the first century of that era all the books of the New Testament had been written. In these books there are numerous references to natural scenery, as hills, mountains, valleys, plains, lakes, rivers, fountains, and pools; to natural productions, as vines, olives, palms, figs, wheat, barley, mustard, and lilies; to well-known animals, as horses, oxen, sheep, goats, camels, dogs, foxes, locusts, doves, sparrows, eagles, and vipers; and all these references are proved to be trustworthy by evidences found in other writings or in the lands of the Bible. Again, there are frequent allusions in the New Testament to the mixed population which then filled the land of Palestine, to Jews, Greeks, Romans, Syrians, Arabians, and strangers from all the known world; to the religious and civil parties which then existed, as Pharisees, Sadducees, Herodians, with the views, customs, prejudices, and passions that distinguish them; to rulers, often mentioned by name, whether they were kings, tetrarchs, governors, centurions, or priests of various ranks; Levites, scribes, lawyers, members of the Sanhedrin, and leaders of the synagogue; and all these allusions are found on examination to be worthy of entire confidence. So too, there are manifold references to products of human industry, as houses, synagogues, ships, jars, baskets, etc.; and in no instance have these references been found incorrect. Thus when the vast number, the incidental character, and the wonderful accuracy of these allusions are considered, it is natural to conclude that the writers of this remarkable book were kept from error by a wisdom higher than their own. A similar conclusion must follow a careful examination of the Old Testament.

3. *The second evidence of its divine origin.* To verify the proposition given above, reference may be made in the second place to prophecy fulfilled. For not only did

the sacred writers profess to record past events; they also predicted future events. To do this with any considerable exactness they must have been taught by one who knows what is to be, as well as what has been. It is perhaps credible that honest and intelligent men should succeed in giving a nearly faultless account of matters within the range of their own observation; it is likewise conceivable that far-seeing statesmen should be able now and then to forecast the destiny of a single tribe or nation; but it is not credible that such predictions as are found in the Scriptures could have been made without divine illumination—predictions concerning *nations,* as Egypt, Edom, Syria, Judea; *cities,* as Nineveh, Babylon, Tyre, Sidon, Jerusalem; and *persons,* as Cyrus, John the Baptist, and Jesus Christ. The argument from prophecy is therefore conclusive as to an important part of the Old Testament, for it establishes most clearly the fact of divine illumination in certain instances, and thus prepares a thoughtful mind to believe it possible in other cases. This argument was frequently used by the early Christians, by the writers of the New Testament, including the apostles, and even by the Lord Jesus himself; yet it was never so strong as it is to-day.

4. *The third evidence of its divine origin.* That the Bible is from God reference may be made, in the third place, to the remarkable originality and consistency of its religious teaching. This teaching relates primarily to the nature of God, to the moral state of man, and to the way of life. To begin with the first of these topics, the sacred writers agree in representing God to be personal, supreme, righteous, and benevolent. None of them speak of God as mere force or law, acting blindly and without choice, but all with a grand uniformity and blessed confidence refer to him as intelligent, wise, and free. They say that he knows, feels, and wills, that he speaks and hears, loves

and hates, legislates and judges, rewards and punishes, adapts means to ends, and rejoices in the work of his hands. The personality of God enters into the very substance and marrow of their doctrine. They also teach that God is supreme. He is the maker of all things, and his word is almighty. He is the upholder of all things, even the forces of nature submit to his behests and work out the councils of his will. Moreover, he is righteons. Justice and judgment are the basis of his throne. The law which emanates from him is holy, and the commandment holy and just and good. There is no truth which the sacred writers assert more positively than the absolute rectitude of God as the sovereign ruler of the universe. Likewise God is benevolent. To this Moses and all the prophets bear witness; to this Christ and his apostles add their testimonies. By the former Jehovah was revealed as "merciful and gracious," long-suffering and abundant in goodness and truth, forgiving iniquity, transgression, and sin, and by the latter, as one who "so loved the world that he gave his only begotten Son that whosoever believeth in him should not perish but have eternal life." This in brief is the biblical doctrine of God. He is personal, supreme, righteous, and benevolent. And he is such according to the testimony of the earliest books as well as the latest. There is progress in the revelation of the divine character, but all of them bear witness to the facts named above.

Again, the sacred writers agree throughout in their account of the moral state of man. They all bear witness to his sinfulness; they all affirm his guilt. He is not unfortunate, but culpable. The evils to which he is subjcet are the fruit of his disobedience to a holy law. Sin is universal, and all men are therefore guilty in the sight of God. This is their teaching from Genesis to Revelation. There is the same agreement among the sacred writers in their doctrine of "the way of life." This has been denied, but without any valid reason. The more carefully one searches the Scriptures, as a progressive revelation of saving truth, the more clearly will he see that they everywhere ascribe salvation to the grace of God. But the idea of grace presupposes that of justice, and justice cannot be disregarded in the exercise of grace. Both are divine and both must be honored. Accordingly the ritual of sacrifice in the Mosaic economy represented the same principle which rules in the vicarious death of Christ. The sixteenth chapter of Leviticus, the fifty-third chapter of Isaiah, and the ninth and tenth of the Epistle to the Hebrews, prove when compared, that the way of life revealed by Moses and the prophets was the same in principle as that revealed by Christ and his apostles; yea more, they prove that the earlier sacrifices were, in a pictorial way, types of the one effectual sacrifice offered by Christ.

5. *The fourth evidence of its divine origin.* That the Bible is from God may be concluded, in the fourth place, from the character of Christ as set forth in the New Testament. It has been seen of late as never before that the Christian religion has its center in the person of Jesus of Nazareth, and that it is only necessary to study without prejudice the records of his life in order to be convinced of the truth of that religion. For the existence of the records can never be accounted for without assuming the existence of him whose person and work they describe. The reason for this statement cannot indeed be given at length, but a few remarks will put the reader's mind in contact with some of them. First, the character of Christ is at once faultless and superhuman. It is faultless; every attempt to discover a blemish in it has failed. The keen eye of criticism has searched eagerly for the slightest proof of evil, but has searched in vain, yet more than this must be said: the character of Christ is superhuman. According

to the New Testament, while truly man, he was far more than man. He was divine as well as human, a being of transcendent power, love, and grace, walking upon the earth, but having commerce with the skies; the unseen and infinite were visible to him, and he was in the bosom of the Father whom he declared. The forces of nature obeyed his will; life and death owned his authority; and spirits of evil confessed him Lord. This blending of the natural with the supernatural, of the human with the divine, without a note of real discord or a sign of actual conflict is the miracle of the Saviour's character as set forth in the Gospels; and it can never be explained without assuming as a fact the existence of Christ in Palestine at the beginning of our era. Again, the character of Jesus is one that rises above all national or sectarian bias; it is purely and broadly human. Whatever he may have been in body, in spirit he was neither a Semite nor an Aryan, neither a Jew nor a Greek, neither a Pharisee nor a Sadducee, but in the largest and highest sense of the word a man. Nothing truly human was alien to him. It is absurd, therefore, to suppose that a Jew living then could have originated, by the simple force of imagination, such a character and set it before the world in such a narrative as that of either of the four Gospels. Besides, it must be borne in mind that the Jews were neither expecting nor desiring such a Messiah as Jesus of Nazareth is said to have been. They were looking for a temporal prince.

In conclusion, the divine origin of the Bible rests upon a sure foundation, and may be taught without fear of error. The accuracy of its language in statements not strictly religious; the fulfilment of many of its predictions; the originality and consistency of its religious teaching; and the faultless superhuman character of Christ are parts of this solid foundation, and parts of such strength as to make our confidence in the whole reasonable. The Bible, rightly interpreted, is the word of God to men, and not one jot or tittle of it will fail.

Topics for Class Discussion

1. How the Bible came from God.
2. Some evidences of the divine origin of the Bible.
3. The greatest evidence of its divine origin.
4. Objections to the divine origin of the Bible.
5. Religious experience and the divine origin of the Bible.

Topics for Class Papers

1. Evidences of the divine origin of the Bible.
2. The nature and extent of inspiration.

LESSON III

THE HUMAN ELEMENT IN THE BIBLE

Reference literature. Geistweit, "The Young Christian and His Bible"; Conley, "The Bible in Modern Light"; Hazard-Fowler, "The Books of the Bible"; Kent, "The Origin and Permanent Value of the Old Testament."

1. *The Bible came through man.* We have seen that the Bible came *from* God. It is equally important for us to see that the Bible came *through* man. It was written by men. Holy men spoke and wrote as they were moved by the Spirit. Yet this divine guidance did not take from them their human nature, nor do away with their personal feelings or their mental traits. One easily becomes familiar with the spirit and style of some of its writers. To a large extent the Bible is the outgrowth of the religious experiences and hopes of good men. The writers of this remarkable book tell us what their own eyes have seen, what their own minds have thought, and what their own hearts have felt about the deep things of God and religion. In its essence religious experience is about the same in all ages, but the conceptions and expressions of that experience differ according to race, times, and conditions. Hence there is growth of thought in the Bible. It is a progressive revelation. There is growth because religious experience is ever growing. Religion is not a static thing. The truth is revealed to man as man is open to receive it. Thus God uses the law of accommodation in revealing himself to men.

2. *The writers of the Bible saw truth from different points of view.* No one would think of denying this to-

day. Only God sees truth in the absolute. Man is ever limited in his conception of truth. God gave to the various writers their message, but it comes to us with a coloring of their own personalities. They were not mere reporters; they were interpreters. As we have seen in Lesson I, Matthew's view of Christ is not Mark's; nor was Luke's that of John. Paul does not see all things as Peter; indeed, there is a freedom in Paul's thought that knows no bounds save the consciousness that God is leading him. He loves to refer to his own experiences, and occasionally offers his own personal judgment on matters. Furthermore, some of the Bible writers saw deeper into religious truth than others. Here again each had his own message according to the gift of God and the measure of his own being; but the message of some was greater and deeper than that of others. In Isaiah in the Old Testament and in Paul and John in the New religious truth found its deepest expression. One of the glories of the Bible is that God conveyed his message through many different kinds of men, some great and some small. Thus the truth finds points of contact with men in every walk of life.

3. *The writers of the Bible used sources.* Some of the books of the Bible as we now have them are made up of earlier documents. Bible scholars in general to-day hold that the book of Genesis is to some extent a compilation. Moses doubtless used both traditions and earlier writings in the making of this book. The larger part of the other books of the Pentateuch came from Moses, though it is now held by even the most conservative scholars that there were additions here and there by later hands. An example of this is the account of Moses' death in Deuteronomy. Parts of the book of Leviticus also were of later date. The highly developed ritual of that book was more than likely a growth. Here and there in the Old Testament the writers refer to books not found

in the Bible. In Josh. 10 : 13 we have a reference to the book of Jasher; so also in 2 Sam. 1 : 18. In 1 Chron. 29 : 29 the history of Nathan is mentioned. 2 Chron. 9 : 29 refers to the prophecy of Ahijah (for others see Geistweit's "The Young Christian and His Bible," p. 56). In the New Testament we know that Matthew and Luke used sources in the writing of their Gospels. Luke, in the preface of his Gospel, practically claims to have used the narratives drawn up by other hands. Two of the sources they used were the Gospel of Mark, for this was the earliest Gospel written, and the Logia. The Logia was a book of the sayings of Jesus, and perhaps furnished the basis for the sermonic arrangement of Matthew. Some claim that Luke used sources in the writing of the book of Acts. This, however, is not established. "All this shows sensible human elements, which in no measure detracts from the value of the Bible as a revelation. One may be guided in the use of material as he may be in the matter of original composition."

4. *The human element strengthens the Bible.* The writing of the Bible by men was the natural way. This does not mean that the supernatural is left out. In a sense the supernatural chose the natural. God might have written his revelation with his own hand on the firmament of the heavens, but he did not choose to give it in that way. If the Bible had been dropped down to the earth in some mysterious way it would never have had power over the hearts of men. There would have been a superstition about the book that would have made it an idol, and its purpose would thus have been defeated. The fact that the Bible came through the mind of man enables the mind of man to see something of its meaning. It is said: "If you tell us what your own eyes have seen and what your own heart has felt, then you will have power over us, and not until then." The Bible writers do this, and hence

no book has ever won such power over the hearts of men. As Coleridge says, "It finds us." There is a ring of reality in its utterances that makes men feel that God is speaking to them out of the experiences and hopes of its writers. In the making of the Bible God used the forms of thought common to man. Thus man is able to understand, *apperceive,* the thoughts of the Bible. Thus points of contact are established between God and man through man. Again, God used the sympathy of men in the making of the Bible. The Bible writers come to us with love and sympathy and tell us that God's attitude toward us is one of love and sympathy; only his love is infinitely above theirs. Thus the Bible becomes God's love-letter to man. In it the hungering of the human heart for sympathy, fellowship, and love meets the One who is able and ready to bestow them all. When God wanted man to see this fully and clearly he sent his own Son clothed in the form of mankind. Only as God reveals himself through the human can the human ever understand God. "It is not therefore the human element in the Bible which operates against its being a divine revelation." That element, when properly understood, always and everywhere strengthens the Bible as the message of God to men.

Topics for Class Discussion

1. Religious experience and the writing of the Bible.
2. Some human elements in the Bible.
3. The different view-points of the Bible writers.
4. The use of sources in the writing of the Bible.
5. How the human element in the Bible finds us.

Topics for Class Papers

1. The human and divine in religion.
2. How the human element strengthens the Bible.

LESSON IV

BIBLE HISTORY AND CHRONOLOGY

Alvah Hovey, D. D., LL. D.

Reference literature. Hovey, "The Bible"; Nordell, "Studies in Old Testament History"; Taylor, "Historical Books of the Old Testament"; Smith, "Old Testament History"; Nordell, "Studies in the Apostolic Age"; Gilbert, "A Short History of the Apostolic Age."

1. *General outline.* In Lesson I we have seen that the Bible contains historical literature. "As compared with other sacred books, *e. g.*, the Koran, the Avesta, the Vedas—no feature of the Bible is more distinctive or noteworthy than the place which it gives to authentic history. The word of God has a solid and tangible setting in the affairs of men. The record is careful to state the circumstances that precede, and attend, and follow after a divine message, and these circumstances aid us in testing the record, in interpreting the message, and in deciding whether it was really from God. Besides this they increased the power of the Bible over the mass of the people a hundredfold. Yet history is not the end of the Bible. The course of human events is narrated only so far as it conditions a special revelation of God to mankind. The living heart of the Bible is the supernatural and saving grace of God through Christ, while its human history is but the visible form which reveals the action of that throbbing heart. Hence biblical history follows the track of divine revelation. Here it is personal, there tribal, and farther on national, but everywhere subordinate to the higher and

religious principle of the record. This must be steadily borne in mind by one who desires to understand biblical history and appreciate its value.

This history may be naturally divided into three great periods, extending from the creation of Adam to the death of Moses, from the death of Moses to the birth of Christ, and from the birth of Christ to the close of the New Testament, A. D. 100. On the lowest computation the first period covers about twenty-five hundred years, the second about sixteen hundred, and the third about one hundred. The periods as given above are frequently named the Patriarchal, the Mosaic, and the Christian.

2. *The first period.* The first period is from Adam to the death of Moses. The history of this period is given in the first five books of the Old Testament. After a sublime vision of the creation of all things by the word of God, the holy narrative confines itself to the story of man. He was made in the image of God, intelligent, free, upright—man first and woman from man. The holy pair were placed in a garden, of whose fruits they were to eat with one exception. By that exception their fidelity was tested and found wanting. Thus sin entered and the unhappy pair were driven out of the garden, but not without a ray of light from the Holy One in the promise of a coming Redeemer. Now follows the well-known story of Cain and Abel, and the selection of Seth as the father of the "sons of God." The sons of Seth, however, took their wives of the daughters of Cain, and the result was a progeny more wicked than any that had gone before. True religion waned, and at last no more than a single household remained true to Jehovah, so after a warning of one hundred and twenty years the deluge was sent, and all but the family of Noah perished. From the family of Noah the human race started on a new career, but the folly of the patriarch and the mockery of his sons proved

that sin had not perished in the flood. Yet God was pleased to establish his covenant with Noah, giving promise of special blessings, first to the line of Shem, and through that to the line of Japhet. But sin continued, as is seen in the building of the tower of Babel. With a lapse of a few centuries the majority of the people had turned to the service of "other gods." Then follows the story of the call of Abraham, and the selection of the chosen family through which the religion of Jehovah was to be preserved in the earth, and made a blessing finally to all the nations. Abraham, Isaac, and Jacob are the earliest custodians of this blessing. The book of Genesis closes with the chosen people in Egypt and the beautiful story of Joseph. For about two hundred years they rapidly increased in numbers and wealth, until at length they began to be feared by the Egyptians and their king. Subjection and slavery follows. In time Moses was raised up by Jehovah as their deliverer. God appeared to him and gave him a commission to lead the children of Israel out of Egypt into Canaan. Reluctantly he accepted the commission and demanded of the king liberty for his people. The demand was refused, but the hand of God was against Egypt, and after great signs and wonders had been wrought the king yielded, and Israel went out of the house of bondage—a free people. At Sinai, Jehovah appeared in majesty, and delivered to the infant nation, through Moses, a code of laws—moral, ceremonial, and civil—under which it was to live and prosper. Thus the chosen people seemed to be prepared to take possession of their appointed land. But they were not, hence they were doomed to lead a wandering life in the peninsula of Sinai forty years. Even Moses, the great leader, was not permitted to enter the promised land. He led the people to the borders of it, and then, at the age of one hundred and twenty years, died "in the land of Moab, according to the word of the Lord."

3. *The second period.* The second period is from the death of Moses to the birth of Christ. Soon after the death of Moses, Joshua led the people over Jordan and began the conquest of Palestine. The fortunes of the war were various, but always on the side of Israel when obedient to God. In a few years the whole land was said to be taken, though certain minor parts of it were still held by the former inhabitants. It was all, however, divided by lot, and given as an inheritance to the children of Israel. After the death of Joshua the nation was ruled by judges about four hundred and fifty years. It was a period of many changes, of heroic but fitful patriotism. When the people fell into idolatry they were overpowered and oppressed by their warlike neighbors. When they turned to the Lord he brought deliverance by the hand of judges. The tabernacle was in Shiloh during this period, but the worship was irregular. "Every one did that which was right in his own eyes." Many of the people had no love for Jehovah their king. They clamored for a visible instead of an invisible king. They wished to be like the nations round about. God granted their wish, and Saul was anointed by Samuel and accepted by the nation as king. Saul proved disobedient to God, and at his death the kingdom was transferred to David, a man of Judah, a brave captain, a cunning musician, an inspired poet, and a loyal though not faultless servant of Jehovah. During his reign the nation steadily advanced in power. The reign of his son Solomon was also very prosperous. The temple was built on Moriah, the boundaries of the kingdom enlarged, commerce and arts flourished, and the Israelites were looked upon as a great people. It was the golden age of the nation.

The burdens imposed by Solomon were heavy, and on the accession of his son to the throne the kingdom divided. This division was permanent. The story of both kingdoms is told in the Bible, but the chief interest is with the Southern kingdom. For the worship of Jehovah languished in the Northern kingdom, and not a single king distinguished himself as a true servant of Jehovah. The tendency was ever downward till the end came. On the other hand, the kingdom of Judah lasted longer—three hundred and eighty-nine years. Its kings were all of Davidic stock, and some of them were devout servants of Jehovah. Its temple was in Jerusalem. Its prophets were many and faithful, yet there was a strong tendency to irreligion and idolatry. The end came with the deportation into Babylon, 586 B. C.

Concerning the mass of the Jews during the seventy years of their captivity little is said. Interesting notices of this period, however, may be found in Jeremiah, Ezekiel, and Daniel. Daniel set himself to pray for the deliverance of his people, and Cyrus, the conqueror of Babylon and king of Persia, issued a decree permitting the Jews to return to the Holy Land and rebuild the temple. About fifty thousand returned under this decree. Eighty-seven years later another company returned, and thirteen years after this still another. The exile seems to have cured the Jews of their ancient longing after idolatry. For a knowledge of the history of the Palestinian Jews during the four hundred years next preceding the birth of Christ, uninspired records must be consulted; and of these the most reliable are the first book of the Maccabees and the writings of Josephus.

4. *The third period.* This period is from the birth of Christ to the end of the first century. The history given by the New Testament describes the founding of a new religious economy, a spiritual State, which is to fill the whole earth with Christian churches. And the history of this great transaction falls naturally into two parts, which are separated by the outpouring of the Spirit on the day

of Pentecost. For previous to that event Christ began the work in his own person, and subsequently to that event he carried it on to completion by the agency of his inspired apostles. The four Gospels tell the story from different points of view of the life and teachings of Jesus the Christ. Born in Bethlehem, he lived hidden from the world for some thirty years. When about thirty, Jesus came to the Jordan and was baptized by John the Baptist. This done, after a period of trial in the desert, he entered upon the work of teaching and gaining disciples. His teaching was spiritual and profound, yet simple and practical, and largely by means of parables. It thus drew to him the humble, the teachable, the right-minded; but it roused the enmity of the proud and disappointed the hopes of the ambitious. This led to his death on the cross. Being conqueror of death, he rose from the dead and appeared to a few of his disciples, and then ascended to the right hand of God his Father. After ten days the Pentecost came, and the apostles were endued with power from on high. They began at once to declare the way of life to the chosen people. Persecution soon arose, and the disciples were scattered abroad, but wherever they went they preached the word. Paul, a young man of strict integrity, was raised up to be a chosen vessel to bear the truth to the Gentiles. Nothing could surpass his energy, enterprise, firmness, flexibility, self-denial. He preached Christ in Syria, Asia Minor, Macedonia, Achaia, and Rome. No apostle did so much by his voice and pen for the spread of the gospel. Those who were apostles before him labored for the most part with their own people; but not exclusively, for John is said to have lived and taught many years, until near the close of the century, in Ephesus, and Peter seems to have preached the good news with effect in Babylon, if not also in Rome. Others likewise went to places outside of Palestine, and all declared the truth with such zeal that at the end of the first century almost every part of the known world had been reached.

Topics for Class Discussion

1. The historical setting of divine truth.
2. The three great periods in Bible history.
3. The most distinguished men in the first period.
4. Sources of information for the second period.
5. The contribution of the third period to the world's history.

Topics for Class Papers

1. The Bible as a book of history.
2. The contribution of the Jews to civilization.

LESSON V

THE OLD TESTAMENT BOOKS WITH RELATION TO THEIR PLACE IN HISTORY

Reference literature. Hazard-Fowler, " The Books of the Bible with Relation to Their Place in History "; Hamill, " The Books of the Bible "; Rowland, " The Pentateuch "; Taylor, " Historical Books of the Old Testament "; Pidge, " The Prophetical Books of the Old Testament "; Orr, " The Problem of the Old Testament "; any good introduction to the Bible.

1. *The books grouped.* The Old Testament books are the product of a long period of divine revelation. The writing of these books covered perhaps a period of a thousand years or more. They fall naturally into groups. " In the English Bible they are arranged, not in the order in which they appear in the Hebrew Bible, but in that assigned to them by the Greek translation. In this translation the books are grouped according to their contents—first, historical books, then the poetical, and lastly the prophetical." (McFadyen.) In the Hebrew Bible we have a triple division into law, prophets, and writings. This arrangement probably represents the history of the Old Testament canon, the law or Pentateuch being the first canon to which the prophets, including the historical books, Joshua to Kings, were later added, while the remaining books came later to be classed with the sacred books. Neither the Hebrew nor the English Bible arranges the books in the order of time and authorship. In this study we shall arrange the books into four groups, as in Lesson I; that is, as follows: The legal books, the historical books, the poetical books, and the prophetical books. We shall take up each of these groups in order

and seek to indicate the place of each book in the stream of history, giving the name of the possible author.

2. *Group I—the legal books.* There are five of these books, and for this reason they are commonly called the Pentateuch, a Greek combination, meaning "five books." They are as a whole the earliest books of the Bible, parts of them going back in the form of documents to the times even before Moses. Genesis, the first of these books, is the "book of beginnings"; of the world, of man, of sin, of redemption. It begins with the creation and traces the work of God, first for the whole human family and then with the chosen people, through whom he is to bless the world, closing with that people in Egypt under the glorious protectorship of Joseph. It was doubtless compiled by Moses, from traditions and documents current in his day. The book as we have it is a unity, though that does not argue that it was first written by one hand, nor that parts of it may not have been added by a later hand. Exodus tells the story of the bondage in Egypt and the "way out" to the law and to the organization of the people as a nation under Moses. There is no reason to doubt if the exodus be a fact and was under the direction of Moses, that he should have written the book very much as we have it. Leviticus likewise belongs to the wilderness age of Israel, and the essential forms of worship in it may well belong to that age. It is likely, however, that the book is a growth, and that the highly developed ritual in it was the progressive expression of the religious life of Israel through many years. The book of Numbers continues the history laid down by Exodus. Exodus closes with the rearing of the tabernacle in the Sinaitic plain, while Numbers opens with a census of the tribes a month later. It tells the story of the wilderness wanderings, bringing the narrative forward to the plains east of Jordan, where a portion of Israel settled permanently. The

narrative is dropped here ready to be resumed in Joshua and Judges. There is no good reason to doubt that the larger part of the book came from the hand of Moses. Deuteronomy, the last book of the Pentateuch, contains for the most part a restatement of the Mosaic legislation. In form it is a series of discourses addressed to the people. It was produced just before the days of Moses were numbered, and when Israel was on the point of invading Canaan. Parts of it, like the last chapter, were added by later hands. The book as a whole gives the impression of having been written by an eye-witness. Thus we may conclude that the legal books in their larger part go back to the time of Moses, fourteen to fifteen hundred years before Christ. When we say this we leave room for additions by later hands. In this sense the books were a growth.

3. *Group II—the historical books.* The historical books run from Joshua to Esther—twelve in number. There are two kinds of histories—the prophetic and the priestly. Roughly speaking, the prophetic histories are Joshua to 2 Kings, and the priestly histories 1 Chronicles to Esther. In places both cover the same matter. The earlier histories are the prophetic, beginning with Joshua. The book of Joshua continues the narrative of the Pentateuch. It tells the story of the conquest of Canaan, and of the allotment of that land to the tribes of Israel, closing with two farewell addresses of a hortatory nature. The book bears the name of Joshua rather because he is its central figure rather than its author. The Jewish tradition was that Joshua followed the example of Moses, and under divine command wrote the annals of his own time. Some, however, attribute the main part of the book to him only; others attribute it to an unknown writer of the time of Saul, and others still to a compilation in the time of David. It is said of Joshua's own address that "he wrote these

words in the book of the law of God." It is entirely probable that parts of the book were from his hands. The exact date and the name of its author cannot be given. "Judges, so entitled because it tells of Israel's non-regal rulers, and Ruth, bearing the name of its chief character, were considered one book in the Jewish canon, and said to be the work of Samuel. In them we have the earliest sketches of what is properly the national history of Israel, extending over a period of about three centuries from the death of Joshua to the birth of Samuel." (Moore.) 1 and 2 Samuel were also one book in the Hebrew Bible. 1 Samuel opens with a scene still with the ages of the judges, and carries the history through the entire age of Samuel, the reign of Saul, the rise of David to the position of a great warrior, closing with the death of Saul and his three sons. 2 Samuel opens with David's receipt of the news of this disaster, and with his beautiful elegy upon them. It includes David's rise to rule over all Israel, and substantially his entire reign. These books come to us from an unknown author, and date, perhaps, from soon after the disruption of the kingdom. These books are composite in character. The name Samuel was given to them, doubtless, because of the large part Samuel played in the reorganization of the people. The last two books of the prophetic histories are 1 and 2 Kings. These were originally one book. They were compiled by an unknown author or authors. They are referred to Jeremiah, Ezra, and others. The exact date of their composition is not known. The books begin with the death of David, about 1000 B. C., and close with the captivity of Judah, 586 B. C., thus covering a period of four hundred and twenty-seven years—the longest and most eventful period of the Jewish national life. During the latter half of this period most of the prophetical books of the Old Testament were written.

The priestly histories begin with the Chronicles. These books were originally one, under the title of "Annals of Days"; in the Septuagint they were separated and termed "Things Omitted"; and in the Vulgate styled "Chronica," whence the title in our English Bible. The compiler, thought to be Ezra, drew upon many sources in the composition of this history. "In a way these are parallel with the entire series of the prophetic histories. They begin with Adam and continue even later than Kings. The materials, however, from Adam to Saul consist of little more than genealogical matter; the historical narrative beginning with Saul's death. This point of beginning suggests instantly the purpose of the history. It is in the line of David and the history associated with it, especially the temple history, in which the Chronica is primarily interested. Northern Israel is left out of the history, except when in direct contact with Judah, and the priests and Levites are made much more prominent than in Samuel and the Kings." (Fowler.) The book of Ezra opens with a story of the return from exile under the decree of Cyrus the Great, and of the rebuilding and dedication of the temple. The second part recounts the mission and reforms of Ezra himself a half century later—458 B. C. The book of Nehemiah records the two visits of Nehemiah to Jerusalem—445 and 432 B. C.—with the rebuilding of the walls, and includes an account of the reading of the law and the renewing of the covenant with Jehovah, in which Ezra is the chief figure. These two books were one in the Hebrew canon. They were doubtless written by the two persons whose names they bear. The story of Esther is laid in the period between the rebuilding of the temple and the mission of Ezra, and has for its scene of action the seat of the Persian government far away from Palestine.

4. *Group III—the poetical books.* These poetical books

are six in number—Job, Psalms, Proverbs, Ecclesiastes, Song of Solomon, and Lamentations. They have no such clear and immediate connection with the history as the legal and prophetical books. It is difficult, therefore, to fix their dates and name the authors. The book of Job is a drama setting forth the struggles of a devout soul over the "hardest of human problems—why should the good be called to suffer." The book is called Job, not because he is its author, but because he is the central figure in it. Once it was considered the oldest book in the Bible, the Jews attributing it to Moses. Some assign it to an unknown author in the reign of Solomon. Many scholars now place it after the exile. Psalms is the prayer and praise book of the Hebrews. The ancient Jews assign the authorship of most of the psalms, and the compilation of the book to David, while the tendency to-day is just the opposite. The book contains poems, probably dating from the age of Moses to a time much later than that of Ezra and Nehemiah. It is thus a collection of many of Israel's poetic writers, and must therefore have been completed at a very late date in Hebrew history. It is made up of smaller and earlier collections of various dates, and doubtless the principal collection was the work of David. In this book almost all aspects of Old Testament experience and teachings are reflected in poetic expression.

The book of Proverbs contains the practical philosophy of ancient Israel, stated in Hebrew parallelisms, the principal form of Hebrew poetry. It is confessedly a collection of wisdom gathered from various thinkers. It had, therefore, a long and gradual growth, and doubtless many of "the wise" men of Israel made contributions to it. "The first verse of the book names as author Solomon the king; but as the book of Psalms is named after David, the chief contributor, so it is with Proverbs. Solomon, perhaps, wrote more than all others whose proverbs enter into the book." (Hamill.) He doubtless made the first collection of these proverbs, though its present form belongs to a later age. Ecclesiastes has been called the pessimistic book of the Bible. though to the writer it is falsely so called. It deals with the problem of "the highest good," and shows that this cannot be found in the material things of earth, but in the fear of God and obedience to his command. Thus no book of the Bible is truer to life than Ecclesiastes. The point is that apart from God nothing satisfies; hence man, to be happy, must come into harmony with God. The book is attributed to Solomon, and whether he be the author or not no man was more able than he by experience to come to such a conclusion. The book may well, therefore, belong to him. The Song of Solomon is a song of true love. "In this book Solomon appears as a character participating in the action rather than as the author, and the date of writing is highly uncertain. We cannot therefore consider it in relation to its place in history." (Fowler.) The book of Lamentations belongs to the opening years of the exile, and is a collection of five elegies, expressing in artistic form sorrow over the wretched condition of Jerusalem, "The book was by the Jews very appropriately set apart for public reading on the anniversary of the destruction of the first temple." It was written by Jeremiah.

5. *Group IV—the prophetical books.* These books are usually divided into major and minor prophets. This distinction is based upon the mere length of the books, and hence is of no value. There are sixteen of the prophetical books. Just when the prophets arose is not known. Some trace them back to the earliest times, even in Egypt before the exodus. (Breasted.) It is commonly held that they were organized into schools in the days of Samuel. The first prophets of note after Moses in the Bible are Elijah and Elisha. If they left any writings these writings

do not bear their names. The earliest written prophetic message we have is doubtless found in the book of Amos. From this point forward we have the words of the prophets written down by themselves or their immediate followers. Amos delivered his prophecies along about the year 750 B. C. He was a native of the Southern kingdom, living as a herdsman at Tekoa, a few miles south of Bethlehem; but he prophesied at Bethel, in the Northern kingdom, where he predicted the downfall of the dynasty of Jeroboam II. The Prophet Hosea preached also in northern Israel and only a few years later than Amos—745-735 B. C. The opening chapters of Hosea fall within the prosperons era of Jeroboam II, while the remainder of the work seems to have as its background the troublous period immediately after when usurper followed usurper. The book is a good sequel to Amos. The next prophet in order of time is Isaiah, who began his work probably about 734 B. C. A dozen years later Samaria was captured and northern Israel destroyed by Assyria. Twenty years after, in the reign of Hezekiah, Judah, having rebelled against Assyria, was devastated and Jerusalem was saved only by the providential destruction of the army of Sennacherib. Through these years of frequent crises Isaiah, preacher, poet, and statesman, was ever at hand with the message of God. The latter portion of the book of Isaiah does not seem to fit in with this period, and by many scholars is referred to the later years of exile. "The book of Micah is the fourth and last member of the splendid group of prophecies which belong to the eighth century B. C.—Amos and Hosea in northern Israel, Isaiah and Micah in Judah. In a measure Micah is the counterpart of Amos." "In chronological order Nahum follows Isaiah, Micah having been contemporary with the great evangelical prophet. The only certain clue to Nahum's date is his reference to the taking of Thebes, which we learn from the Assyrian monument, took place in 665 B. C. He prophesied thus in the reign of Manasseh. Of the sins and dangers of Judah he says not a word. His burden is the doom that hangs over the great heathen city of Nineveh." (Pidge.) The prophecy probably belongs to the reign of Josiah before the great reform instituted in the eighteenth year of that reign—621 B. C. The corrupt worship and general wickedness of Manasseh and his people called forth the threatened "Day of the Lord" of Zephaniah. The prophecy of Habakkuk belongs to the time when the Babylonian power is first seen to be the scourge which Jehovah will use in the "Day of the Lord," probably about 600 B. C. "The book of Jeremiah contains the messages of that prophet from his call in the thirteenth year of Josiah's reign (626 B. C.) until the flight into Egypt after the destruction of Jerusalem, together with an unusually large amount of biographical material. A large part of it finds its natural setting in the circumstances of the following years, when the party that favored an alliance with Egypt was dominant and Jeremiah was vainly striving to prevent the folly of hostility toward the power of Babylon." (Fowler.) Obadiah's prophecy was a fierce denunciation of Edom for her mistreatment of Jacob, and arose from Edom's readiness to share in the sack of Jerusalem in 586 B. C. It may be dated, therefore, about the year 580. It is here also that the prophecy of Ezekiel first begins. Ezekiel was carried captive with Jehoiachin in 586 B. C. He is thus the great prophet of the exile, holding forth the promise to Israel of future restoration to a purified and more glorious Jerusalem. Twenty years after the close of Ezekiel's work there arose what most scholars to-day call "the great unknown prophet" of the later exile, whose ministry of hope is recorded in Isa. 40 to 66, about 550 B. C. Haggai and Zechariah are the first prophets of the restoration. Their prophecies are concerned wholly with the rebuilding of the temple (520-516 B. C.). Malachi is chiefly occupied with proper provision for the temple service, and the suppression of foreign marriages. It thus connects itself closely with the reform measures of Ezra and Nehemiah, and is probably dated during the period 458-432 B. C.

It will be observed that three of the prophets have not been accounted for so far—Joel, Jonah, and Daniel. The finding of their places in the stream of history is not easy. Some put Joel as the first of the prophets, about 800 B. C., with Jonah following, at 780 B. C. Most scholars of to-day, however, place them much later—after the date of the exile. The question of their date is therefore an open question. The same is true of the book of Daniel. Its apocalyptic tendencies suggest that it is perhaps the latest of the Old Testament books, though many scholars place it much earlier.

Topics for Class Discussion

1. The earliest books of the Old Testament.
2. Which group of books on the whole is the oldest.
3. Compare the prophetic history and the priestly history as to time.
4. Name the prophetical books in the order of time.
5. Which of the poetical books is the oldest and which the latest.

Topics for Class Papers

1. The legal books of the Old Testament.
2. The prophet and the prophetical books in Israel's history.

LESSON VI

THE BOOKS OF THE NEW TESTAMENT WITH RELATION TO THEIR PLACE IN HISTORY

Reference literature. Burton, " A Short Introduction to the Gospels "; Burton, " A Hand Book on the Life of Paul "; Hazard-Fowler, " The Books of the Bible "; Burton, " Records and Letters of the Apostolic Age "; any good introduction to the New Testament.

1. *The books grouped.* It was said in the previous lesson that the Old Testament books were the product of a long period of divine revelation. Not so with those of the New Testament. They are the product of the first expression of Christian inspiration and zeal, all of them being written by the end of the first century A. D. Like the Old Testament books they were written by many different men. Among these writers are the Apostles Matthew, John, Peter, and Paul, the evangelist John Mark, the physician Luke, and others. At first these books were widely scattered, originating in different regions of the great Roman empire, and in many cases were originally sent to individuals and churches in many different districts. The collection of these scattered books into our present New Testament and the sifting out of those early Christian writings that were finally excluded from the canon adopted by the church was a gradual process, as we have already seen. But by the end of the second century these books of the New Testament as we now have it were recognized and appealed to as authorities.

The literary form of the New Testament writings is not so rich in variety as that found in the Old Testament writings. There is very little poetry in the New

Testament, unless we see in the teachings of Jesus in some of his sermons the Hebrew parallel. The principal classes of prose literature are found in abundance—historical narrative, oratory, parable, and philosophical writings. According to their contents the books of the New Testament may be grouped into historical, epistolary, apocalyptic. The epistles may be divided into two classes—the Pauline and the general. The book of Revelation stands by itself, being apocalyptic in character.

2. *Group I—the historical books.* There are five historical books—Matthew, Mark, Luke, John, and Acts. The order of the writing of these books, in point of time, is as follows: Mark, Matthew, Luke, Acts, and John. The first three Gospels are called the Synoptic Gospels, because they give a similar outline and view of the life of Christ. The Gospel of John stands apart from this group, "dealing largely with different events in the life of Jesus and presenting the whole theme in a very different way." The book of Acts is a sequel to the Gospel according to Luke, and records the spread of Christianity first among the Jews and later among the Gentiles. The book of Mark was written by John Mark, "at different times a companion of Peter and Paul; a work based in considerable part on the discourses of the Apostle Peter, to which Mark had listened, and in which Peter had related many things concerning the life of Jesus." (Burton.) It is beyond question the oldest of the gospel narratives, being written about A. D. 60-64. The place of writing was doubtless Rome, though Chrysostom attributes it to Alexandria. Matthew, the second Gospel in order of time, was written to show that Jesus was in deed and in truth the promised Messiah. It came from the apostle whose name it bears, and was written about A. D. 68-70. (Bartlett.) There was perhaps an earlier and briefer Gospel by Matthew written in Hebrew. Luke contains the Gospel of the humanitarian

Christ, the friend of sinners everywhere. According to Plummer it was written about A. D. 80. The place of writing is very uncertain—probably somewhere in Asia Minor. It is often spoken of as the Pauline Gospel, from the fact that it was written by the physician and companion of Paul—Luke. The book of Acts, which is the earliest history of the spread of Christianity and the church, is also from the hand of Luke, with some possible exceptions. It was written very soon after his Gospel, somewhere about A. D. 81-82. The Gospel of John is the latest of historical books in the New Testament; some say the latest of all of the New Testament books. It was written by the Apostle John in his old age, and while living at Ephesus, about the year A. D. 94-96. Some parts of it seem to be added by a later hand. John saw deeper into the nature of Christ's person and the meaning of his work than any other New Testament writer, hence his Gospel is not simply a narrative of the deeds and sayings of Jesus, but an interpretation of them.

3. *Group II—the Pauline epistles.* The historical books are not the earliest New Testament books. Paul has given us in his letters the first of these writings. Paul's epistles may be classified into four groups: the Thessalonian group, consisting of 1 and 2 Thessalonians; the great doctrinal group, consisting of Romans, 1 and 2 Corinthians, and Galatians; the prison epistles, consisting of Philippians, Ephesians, Colossians, and Philemon; and the pastoral epistles, consisting of 1 and 2 Timothy and Titus. In point of time 1 and 2 Thessalonians come first. While at Corinth on his second missionary journey Paul wrote the first Epistle to the Church at Thessalonica. Being prevented from revisiting Thessalonica, he sent Timothy to look after the Christians there. Timothy returned with an excellent report (3 : 1-6). The second Epistle seems to have been written soon after the first, and while Paul

was still at Corinth. The date of these epistles is somewhere between A. D. 49-53. The next epistle of Paul is Galatians, the first in point of time in the second group. It was written during Paul's stay at Antioch, after his second missionary journey. The date is therefore about A. D. 54-55. It was written during a crisis in the early church, and to show that Christianity was not to be limited to those who demanded outward forms and symbols as vital elements in their religion, but should be open to all who enter into fellowship with God through faith in Jesus Christ. 1 Corinthians was written near the close of Paul's stay at Ephesus, and thus while he was on his third missionary journey. The date is perhaps A. D. 57. The letter deals chiefly with the evils and questions of the church at Corinth. "Between the first and the second Epistles to the Corinthians Paul had left Ephesus, journeyed northward and crossed over to Macedonia. Great anxiety for the Corinthian church has harassed his spirit, but now Titus has met him with news from Corinth that is in the main favorable. Some, however, are still hostile to Paul and ready to create division." (Fowler.) This seems to furnish the occasion for the second Epistle, which was written about A. D. 58 or 59. The letter to the Romans was written at the close of Paul's third visit to Corinth, and just before his starting for Jerusalem with the Gentile contribution for the poor saints of that city. The date is therefore about the year A. D. 59. This letter is Paul's greatest exposition of his gospel, and to a people whom he had never seen, but whom he expects to visit as soon as possible.

It is some time now before he takes up his pen again. Going to Jerusalem, as stated above, he is arrested, imprisoned, and tried. At his trial he appeals to Rome, and after some time he is carried there to appear before Cæsar. His next letters, therefore, are the prison epistles. The first of these is Philippians. "The letter to the Philippians which we have in our New Testament was written from Rome when Paul was a prisoner there." (Burton.) It was called forth by the gift sent from that church to Paul by Epaphroditus. The date is A. D. 62. Of the remaining prison letters Professor Burton has the following to say: "Several circumstances combine to indicate that the letter to Philemon and that to the Colossians were sent at the same time and to the same place; thus both were written when Paul was a prisoner. And the fact that the same messenger, Tychicus, accompanied the letter to the Ephesians along with that to the Colossians, and is in both commended in almost identical words, together with a strong similarity of the two letters in other respects, makes it practically certain that Ephesians was written and sent at the same time with the two to Colossæ." The date may be put down as A. D. 62-64.

With respect to the pastoral epistles of Paul—1 and 2 Timothy and Titus—it is difficult to find a place for them in the life of Paul unless we hold that Paul was released from the Roman prison mentioned in the last chapter of Acts. The tide of opinion to-day is toward the belief that Paul's life and missionary activity did not end at the point at which the book of Acts closes, but that he was released, and after further missionary labors rearrested and put to death. Hence the opinion is in favor of the genuineness of the pastoral epistles. On this last missionary journey Paul wrote 1 Timothy, doubtless while he was in Macedonia. Later on, at Corinth, he sent his letter to Titus, and on his return to Rome wrote the second letter to Timothy.

4. *Group III—the general epistles and Revelation.* The earliest of the general epistles some scholars say was that bearing the name of James, the brother of our Lord; others, however, place this very late. The date is very

uncertain. 1 Peter purports to come from the Apostle Peter, and was probably written between A. D. 62-67. (Burton.) It was written to encourage suffering Christians to hold fast to the Christianity they had received. 2 Peter, though often denied, was probably written by the apostle whose name it bears. The purpose seems to be the same as in 1 Peter. The date is between A. D. 60 and the death of Peter. The Epistle of Jude professes to come from Judas, brother of James, in all probability the brother of our Lord, and of James, who wrote the Epistle of James. Its date is perhaps A. D. 75 (Zahn), though Weiss places it as early as A. D. 62. The author of Hebrews is unknown, though modern scholars are almost unanimous that it is not from Paul. Its purpose is to convince the readers of the divine origin and finality of Christianity, and so prevent a threatened apostasy. The date is not long before A. D. 70. (Westcott.) The first Epistle of John was written by a personal follower of Jesus, doubtless the Apostle John himself. The purpose of the book was to strengthen Christians in their faith and character, especially as against the influence of certain prevalent errors, notably libertinism and docetism. (Burton.) The date is perhaps about A. D. 80, according to Zahn. The second and third Epistles of John were written by a person who designates himself "the elder," who seems to be the same person as the author of the Gospel and the first Epistle. The purpose of 2 John was to guard those addressed against dangers arising out of false teaching until the writer should come; that of 3 John to encourage Gaius in his generous treatment of certain brethren. The date of these letters is near the close of the second century, if by the Apostle John in his old age.

The book of Revelation stands by itself, being as we have seen apocalyptic in character. The writer styles himself John, the servant of Jesus Christ. This may be the Apostle John, though some ascribe it to a presbyter whose name was John. The book in visionary images portrays the triumph of the truth of the gospel, and so gives strength to the Christian in times of persecution and temptation. It is possibly the latest book of the New Testament. The great German scholar Zahn places it at about A. D. 95.

Topics for Class Discussion

1. The origin of the New Testament books in general.
2. The historical books of the New Testament.
3. The history of the Christian church in the book of Acts.
4. The time limits in the writing of the New Testament books.
5. The earliest written books of the New Testament.

Topics for Class Papers

1. The chronological order of the Pauline epistles.
2. The time and place of writing of the four Gospels.

LESSON VII

THE LANDS OF THE BIBLE

Alvah Hovey, D. D., LL. D.

Reference literature. Smith, "Historical Geography of the Holy Land"; Stewart, "The Land of Israel"; Calkin, "Historical Geography of Bible Lands"; Macoun, "The Holy Land in Geography and History," two volumes; Hurlbut, "Manual of Biblical Geography"; Morehead, "Mosaic Institutions."

1. *Countries of the Bible.* The lands of the Bible are comprised between ten degrees and fifty-four degrees east longitude and twenty-seven degrees and forty degrees north latitude. A knowledge of these lands must be of great advantage to the Bible student. Only the barest outline can be given here. In order to assist the memory, it may be well to begin with Palestine, and then pass around from Egypt in the southwest through the countries lying south, east, and north, to those lying northwest of the central region. Palestine, the principle theater of biblical events lies nearly in the center of the countries named in the Bible. It is one hundred and forty miles long and forty miles in average breadth, about the size of Massachusetts. It is a land of hills, of plains, and torrent beds. Next to Palestine in importance to the Biblical scholar is the land of Mizraim or Egypt, southwest of Palestine. It is the great valley watered by the Nile, having an area the same as Connecticut. Goshen was in the lower or northern part of the valley. East of Egypt and south of Palestine is the peninsula of Sinai, where the law was given through Moses and where the children of Israel wandered for forty years. East of the northern plateau of Sinai are the mountains of

Edom, and eastward still the wide desert of Arabia, with the head of the Persian Gulf beyond. Lying north of Edom and east of the Dead Sea is the land of Moab; north of Moab and east of the Jordan, the land of Gilead; and north of Gilead, Bashan; and then Syria including Damascus sweeping round to the north of Palestine. East of Moab, Gilead, Bashan, and Syria, is the desert; and beyond the desert is Chaldea, Assyria, Persia, with Media and Armenia farther north. North and northwest of Syria lie the provinces of Asia Minor; and in the latter direction, though beyond the sea and more to the westward, are Macedonia, Achaia, Italy, and Spain. Add to these the islands of the Mediterranean and most of the countries of the Bible have been noticed.

2. *Seas and rivers.* The seas mentioned in the Bible are those now called the Mediterranean Sea, the Red Sea, the Dead Sea, and the sea of Galilee. In the Bible the Mediterranean is sometimes called the "Hinder Sea," meaning by this expression the Western Sea; sometimes the sea of the Philistines, because the land of the Philistines lay upon its eastern coast; and still oftener the "Great Sea," as contrasted with other bodies of water known to the Israelites. It was thus by way of distinction "the Sea." The Red Sea was once called the "sea of Egypt" but commonly the sea of Sedge because it abounds in seaweed; it lies between Egypt and the peninsula of Sinai. The Dead Sea is called in the Pentateuch and the book of Joshua the "sea of Salt" or the "sea of Arabah," and in the prophets "the Sea" in distinction from the Great Sea. Its length is forty-six miles, and its greatest width ten miles and a third. It is about one thousand three hundred and seventeen feet below the level of the Mediterranean at Jaffa. The sea of Galilee is also called the "lake of Gennesareth," from a plain on its northwestern shore, and the "sea of Tiberias" from a town on the southwestern shore.

Shaped like a pear, it is about twelve miles long by seven broad. This lake is between six hundred and seven hundred feet below the level of the Mediterranean. Sudden storms are frequent upon it.

The chief rivers of the Bible are the Jordan, the Nile, and the Euphrates. The Jordan is a remarkable river; rising in Mount Hermon it flows south in cascades of descent about two hundred miles and empties into the Dead Sea. The whole descent from the base of Hermon to the Dead Sea is two thousand and sixteen feet. At the fords opposite Jericho, the river is said to be about forty yards in breadth and ten or twelve feet deep. The current of the river is swift and strong. The Nile is also a remarkable river, and is sometimes called by the sacred writers "the River" or "the River of Egypt." It is nearly four thousand miles long. Egypt owes its fruitfulness to the waters of this river, which overflows its banks during the summer months. The Euphrates is the principle river of western Asia, and is often called "the River" by the Jewish writers. It rises in the mountains of Armenia, and flows south and southeast till it empties into the Persian Gulf. It is mentioned in the Bible as one of the four rivers of Eden, and later as the boundary of the kingdom of Solomon toward the East.

3. *Mountains of the Bible.* With the exception of Ararat in Armenia on which the ark rested while the waters of the flood disappeared, the mountains named in the Bible may be found either in or around Palestine. The western range of Lebanon on the north is continued southward by the central and hilly region of Galilee, of Samaria, and of Judea, ending in the peninsula, while the eastern range is continued by the high hills of Bashan, Moab, and Edom. Between these ranges lie the deep valley of the Jordan, the Dead Sea, and the Arabah. A few of the higher points deserve particular notice. Horeb

and Sinai are of special interest. According to Robinson, Horeb was the name of the central cluster of mountains in the peninsula, and Sinai the name of a single peak in that cluster. Modern usage has reversed this by calling the group Sinai, and the peak Horeb. Next in importance are the "mountains round about Jerusalem," Moriah, Zion, and Olivet. The lowest of these mountains was more than two thousand feet above the level of the sea. The temple of Jehovah stood on Moriah, the palace of David on Zion, and Christ was received up into heaven from the eastern slopes of the mount of Olives. Gerizim and Ebal are twin mountains in the heart of Palestine. According to the command of Moses, when Israel had entered the promised land, six tribes were stationed on the side of Gerizim, facing the northward, to respond to the blessing written in the law, and six tribes on the side of Ebal, facing southward, to respond to the curses of the law, as they were read by Joshua in the valley between. Both of these mountains are terraced and fertile. Carmel is a well-wooded ridge, extending from the sea in a southeasterly direction twelve miles. It terminates at both ends abruptly. The scene of Elijah's conflict with the prophets of Baal is supposed to have been on the eastern declivity of the mountain. Mount Hermon stands at the southern end and is the culminating point of the Anti-Libanus range. It towers high above the ancient border city of Dan, and is the most conspicuous and beautiful mountain in Palestine or Syria. It is ten thousand feet high. Hor and Nebo are memorable as the places on which Moses and Aaron respectively died. The former is on the eastern side of the valley which passes south from the Dead Sea to the gulf of Arabah. Whether Pisgah was the same as Nebo, or a range of mountains with Nebo for one of its summits is not yet decided.

4. *Cities of the Bible.* There are evidences of an early

division of mankind into two classes, those who dwelt in tents and those who dwelt in cities. This division was probably spontaneous. Cain was the first to build a city, or "fenced place," as the Hebrew means. A city was always a walled town, large or small. These walls were for defense from the violence of man. Thus many of the cities of Palestine were built on heights, strong and strategic by nature. "A city set on a hill" was a very common object in the Holy Land. The number of gates and towers in the walls of a fenced city was subject to no rule save that of safety and convenience to the inhabitants. In times of peace the gates were open during the day, but generally closed at night. There were open spaces near the gates, used as places of public resort, and especially for the trial of civil offenses. The streets of Oriental cities are for the most part extremely narrow, and sometimes partly overarched by the projection of the upper story of houses on either side. Some of the streets of Nineveh seem, however, to have been wide enough for chariots to pass each other. To all these fenced cities water was indispensable and great care was taken to provide an abundance of it by means of reservoirs fed by acqueducts from distant sources, and by means of cisterns. No scarcity of water is complained of by Josephus during the terrible and protracted siege of Jerusalem by Titus.

Some of the cities of Palestine of special interest to the Bible student are the priest cities. Forty-eight cities in different parts of the land were assigned to the Levites. Six of these were distinguished as "cities of refuge," three of them, Kadesh, Shechem, and Hebron, being west of the Jordan; and three, Bezer, Ramoth-Gilead, and Golan, east of that river. Sodom and Gomorrah, the "cities of the plain," destroyed by fire from heaven are still matters of wonder. Bethlehem the birthplace of our Lord is prominent in biblical writings. Of course the city of all was the "holy city," Jerusalem. It was the center of the religious life of the people. Jesus wept over it when it did not see the day of its salvation.

5. *Present condition of Bible lands.* Nearly all the Bible countries are far less prosperous, populous, and powerful now than in former times. Once they embraced the civilization of the world; now they are far inferior to many other lands. One is therefore liable to be disappointed by the actual sight of them. This is certainly true of Palestine, with its ruins and desolation on every hand. The change in Egypt is almost as great. The land of "Ham" has long been governed by rulers of foreign extraction, and its people have been overtaxed and disheartened. Instead of ranking with the most powerful nations, the Egyptians are chiefly interesting for what they did before the dawn of Christian civilization. The peninsula of Sinai, and the lands of Edom, Moab, Gilead, Bashan reveal everywhere the same degeneracy; and the predatory Arabs have been charged with being not so much the inhabitants as the makers of the desert. Almost everywhere may be found the footprints of a past greater, wiser, and nobler than the present. Syria, as well as Palestine, and the country east of the Jordan, has suffered the evils of bad government for ages, and her present condition is in no small degree a result of such government, yet parts of it have been accessible to foreigners, and missionaries have sown the seeds of life in many districts of Syria and Armenia. If one turns his eye to the plains of Shinar; to the land of the Chaldeans, the Babylonians, the Assyrians; to the lower banks of the Euphrates, he will discover nothing of interest but ruins; desolation reigns in that region. The same is true to some extent of Asia Minor, or at least of the Christian churches planted in that region. This part of the world has also been under Moslem sway for a very long period, and has experienced the evils inseparable from a bad

government. The same is true of Greece until recently; and the state of Italy is too well known to require description. This sad picture of the present condition of Bible lands agrees wonderfully with the solemn foreshadowings of the Scripture, and therefore justifies our confidence in the truth of Scripture when it foreshadows brighter days for the people of God, both in the life that now is and in that which is to come.

Topics for Class Discussion

1. Location of Bible lands.
2. The most important land mentioned in the Bible.
3. The Jordan River.
4. The geological structure of Palestine.
5. The most important cities of the Bible.

Topics for Class Papers

1. The land of Palestine.
2. Present condition of Bible lands.

LESSON VIII

MANUSCRIPTS AND VERSIONS OF THE BIBLE

Reference literature. Smyth, "How We Got Our Bible"; Pattison, "The History of the English Bible"; Merrill, "The Parchments of the Faith"; Price, "The Ancestry of Our English Bible."

1. *The manuscript sources of the Bible.* "It is a matter of great interest to the Christian to know how he came by his Bible. Here lies a Bible, in its beautiful levant binding, printed on rice paper, in large type—the finest product of the modern printer's and bookbinder's art. Came it so to us from heaven? Came it so to us down the centuries? Was it in this beautiful form that Moses and the prophets left their contributions to it? Is this the book that the apostles and disciples left to us as their legacy? No, our Bible did not come to us a complete volume, dropped from the skies; nor yet was it unearthed as a hidden treasure. It grew as all things with life must grow, and passed through test and trial to the present volume." ("The Young Christian and His Bible," p. 71.) To understand its manuscript sources "let us begin by imagining before us the record chest of one of the early Christian churches—say Jerusalem or Rome or Ephesus—about A. D. 120, when sufficient time had elapsed since the completion of the New Testament writings to allow most of the larger churches to procure copies for themselves. In such a church we should have before us something of this sort: (1) Some manuscripts of the Hebrew Old Testament books. (2) A good many more of the Old Testament books translated into Greek for general use in the churches, Greek being the language most widely used at that time. This translation is called the Septuagint,

or "Version of the Seventy," from an old tradition of its having been prepared by seventy learned Jews of Alexandria. (3) A few rolls of the Apocryphal books. (4) Either the originals or direct copies of the Gospels and the Acts, the Epistles of Paul and Peter and John, and the book of Revelation. Now let us remember clearly that as we look into that old record chest of nearly eighteen hundred years ago we have before us all the sources from which we get our Bible. These writings were of course all manuscript, *i. e.*, written by the hand." (Smyth's "How We Got Our Bible," pp. 9, 10.)

2. *The lost manuscripts.* All the manuscripts in that old record chest, into which we have just looked, have been lost. So far as known no original manuscript of any book of the Bible is in existence. As to the Old Testament whatever Moses and the prophets wrote with their own hands had perished long before the days of Christ. It is not likely that an original copy of the revised version of the Old Testament by Ezra and his immediate followers was even in existence at that day. All the Jews had were copies of the originals. The Greek version of course was a translation. But whatever copies of the Hebrew Bible the Jews had in the apostolic age have long been lost to us. Indeed the earliest Hebrew manuscripts of the Old Testament that we possess date no earlier than about the tenth century. This loss of earlier manuscripts is largely due to the Jewish custom of destroying or burying worn-out manuscripts. And yet we doubtless have a pretty correct copy of the original manuscripts in the Hebrew Bible of to-day. This is due to the careful copying and constant revision of Hebrew scholars. "As far as we can learn there seems to have been a gradual rough sort of revision of the Palestine manuscripts continually going on almost from the days of Ezra. About a thousand years ago this process of Hebrew manuscript revisions came to an end, and thus at that

early date the Hebrew Old Testament was made as nearly correct as the best scholarship of the Jewish academies could make it, after which the older manuscripts gradually disappeared.

As to the New Testament we have manuscripts dating farther back than those of the Old Testament, but we have no writing that dates back to the apostolic age. All those manuscripts of Paul, Peter, John, and others, which we saw in the library of that early church have perished. What we have are copies of these originals. Hence, it is impossible to-day for our eyes to look upon the word of God in the handwriting of those holy men through whom it came to us. Still there is no good reason to doubt but that we have the message of God very much as it was given to them.

3. *The oldest manuscripts of the Bible.* The oldest manuscripts of the Bible which we now have date from about the fourth century of our era. There are three of them. "These three oldest manuscripts are curiously enough in possession of the three great branches of the Christian Church. The ALEXANDRIAN (called for shortness *Codex A*) belongs to Protestant England, and is kept in the manuscript room of the British Museum; the VATICAN (*Codex B*) is in the Vatican Library at Rome; and the SINAITIC (*Codex Aleph*), which has only lately been discovered, is one of the treasures of the church at St. Petersburg. These manuscripts show us the Bible as it existed soon after the apostolic days." (Smyth.)

(1) The VATICAN manuscript. This is the most ancient. It has lain at least four to five hundred years in the Vatican Library at Rome. The manuscript consists of about seven hundred leaves of the finest vellum, about a foot square, bound together in book form. It is not quite perfect, having lost Gen. 1 to 46, as well as Ps. 105 to 137, and all after Heb. 9 : 14 of the New Testament. The papal

authorities have been very jealous guardians of this manuscript, and for a long time persons capable of examining it aright were refused access to it. However, it has of late years become easily accessible with the excellent fac-similes made by order of Pope Pius IX, which may be seen in our chief public libraries.

(2) The SINAITIC manuscript. There is no need of describing this celebrated manuscript, which on the whole very much resembles the other; but the story of its discovery about fifty years ago is full of interest. "It is called the Sinaitic manuscript, from the place where it was found by the great German scholar, Doctor Tischendorf, in St. Catherine's Convent at the foot of Mount Sinai. In visiting the library of the convent in the month of May, 1844, he perceived in the middle of the great hall a basketful of old parchments, and the librarian told him that two heaps of similar old documents had already been used for the fires. What was his surprise to find in the basket a number of sheets of a copy of the Septuagint (Greek) Old Testament, the most ancient-looking manuscript he had ever seen. The authorities of the convent allowed him to take away about forty sheets." (Smyth.) Finally, after fifteen years of endeavor, Tischendorf got possession of the manuscript as we now have it; and it is now stored up in the library of St. Petersburg, the greatest treasure which the Greek Church possesses.

(3) The ALEXANDRIAN manuscript. "This youngest of our three great manuscripts has special interest for us, being in the custody of England, and preserved with our great national treasures in the British Museum. It was presented to Charles I by Cyril Lucar, Patriarch of Constantinople, A. D. 1628, and therefore arrived in England seventeen years too late to be of use in preparing our Authorized version. The Arabic inscription on the first sheet, states that it was written "by the hand of Thekla the martyr."

Only ten leaves are missing from the Old Testament part, but the New Testament is much more defective, having lost twenty-five leaves from the beginning of Matthew, two from John, and three from Corinthians. It is written two columns on a page, the Vatican and Sinaitic having respectively three and four. The original can be seen at the British Museum, but copies which exactly represent it are, like those of the other two, kept in our chief public libraries." These manuscripts along with some others are written in *uncials, i. e.,* they are Greek capitals of small size, with no break between the words or sentences, so that the lines look like one long word. "The number of uncials discovered is about one hundred and twenty, but only one of these contains the entire New Testament." Besides the uncials there are many manuscripts called *cursives, i. e.,* they are written in a running hand. These belong to a later time than the uncials, and are therefore of less value.

4. *Versions.* A version of the Bible is a translation into some other than the original languages. There are many of these, this work having been carried on throughout the Christian centuries. We note some of the ancient versions briefly and then pass on to those in our own language. Of the ancient versions "there are the old Syriac Scriptures, which were probably in use about fifty years after the New Testament was written—a version representing very nearly the language of the people among whom our Lord moved. Those discolored parchments beside them are Egyptian, Ethiopic, and Armenian versions, which would be more useful if our scholars understood these languages better; and the beautiful silver-lettered book, with its leaves of purple parchment is the version of Ulfilas, bishop of the fierce Gothic tribe, about A. D. 350. Here are the old Latin, which, with the Syriac, are the earliest of all versions. But what is this version piled in

such enormous numbers, far exceeding that of all the others put together? It is a version which just now should possess very special interest for all English readers—St. Jerome's Latin Vulgate, the great 'Revised version' of the ancient Western Church. No other work has ever had such an influence on the history of the Bible. For more than a thousand years it was the parent of every version of the Scriptures in western Europe, and even now, when the Greek and Hebrew manuscripts are so easily accessible, the Rhemish and Douay Testaments are translations direct from that book. It is the version of the Catholic Church to this day."

When we come to the English versions there are several of great interest to us. Passing over the Anglo-Saxon translations let us note a few of the great English versions referred to above.

(1) Wycliffe's version. John Wycliffe, "The Morning Star of the Reformation," was the first translator of the Bible into English. His struggles against the Church of Rome led him to see the need of the Bible in the language of the people, if any reform was to be accomplished. And by the middle of 1382 he had completed the first English Bible—one hundred and fifty years before Luther. About one-half of the Old Testament is ascribed to Nicholas Hereford, one of the Oxford leaders of the Lollards. Wycliffe's Bible was based on the Latin Vulgate of St. Jerome and preserves the defects in that volume. "About eight years after its completion the whole was revised by Richard Purvey, his curate and intimate friend, whose manuscript is still in the library of Trinity College, Dublin."

(2) Tyndale's version. After Wycliffe, more than a hundred years passed away before we come to another great version of the Bible. During this period printing was invented, and the revival of learning had spread over Europe. Erasmus issued (1516) the first edition of the

Greek Testament, the Hebrew Bible was first printed (1488), and in 1520 came the "Complutensian Polyglot" Bible in the original languages with grammars and vocabulary. At this critical period William Tyndale was raised up, and at an early age won for himself at Oxford a distinguished position for scholarship. He made use of the new instruments in his Bible study and translations. An exile from England on account of persecution, he succeeded in translating a large part of the Bible from the original, sending out in 1525 the first printed New Testament in English, and in 1530, the Pentateuch, and perhaps also the historical books and part of the prophets. "As we have seen already, all the earlier English versions were but translations of a translation, being derived from the Vulgate or older Latin versions. Tyndale for the first time goes back to the original Hebrew and Greek, though the manuscripts accessible in his time were not of much authority as compared with those used by our revisers now."

(3) The great Bible. Tyndale's dying prayer was, "Lord, open the king of England's eyes." This prayer was soon answered. Three years after his death an English Bible was in every parish church. This Bible was the so-called "Great Bible" of 1539, the first English "Authorized version." In reality this was virtually Tyndale's Bible. In these three years three different versions had appeared in England. In 1536 came the Bible of Myles Coverdale. His Bible makes no pretense to being an original translation. And in the New Testament he follows Tyndale very closely. The following year (1537) appeared "Matthew's Bible," prepared really by John Rogers, one of the early reformers. This work was Tyndale's translation pure and simple, with the exception of the latter half of the Old Testament. Shortly after appeared "Taverner's Bible," which was little more than an edition of Matthew's. None of these versions were satisfactory, "so it came to

pass that the Great Bible was set on foot. Cranmer and some of the chief advisers of the king had set their hearts on having a translation that would be really worthy its position as a national Bible. Myles Coverdale was selected to take charge of the work, and after some delay it was published in April, 1539, and was authorized to be used and frequented in every church in the kingdom."

(4) Genevan Bible. The persecutions of Queen Mary's reign drove many reformers to Geneva. Under the leadership of William Whittingham some of these exile scholars translated the Bible, and published it in 1560. Whittingham introduced into English the verse divisions in the Bible. A copy of this Bible was presented to Queen Elizabeth on her entry into London.

(5) The King James Authorized version of 1611. England had at this time three different versions, the Genevan Bible, the Great Bible, and the Bishop's Bible. But none of these was likely to be accepted by the English nation. There was therefore plainly a need for a new version, which, being accepted by all, should form a bond of union between different classes and rival religious communities. In January, 1604, a conference of bishops and clergy was held in the drawing-room of Hampton Court palace, under the presidency of King James himself. Among other subjects of discussion was that of the defectiveness of the two chief translations of Scripture. This led to a new version committee under the patronage of James I. "Fifty-four learned men were selected impartially from High Churchmen and Puritans, as well as from those who represented scholarship totally unconnected with any party. And in addition to this band of appointed revisers, the king also designed to secure the co-operation of every biblical scholar of note in the kingdom. About three years was spent on the task. A very full and careful use was made of the work that had gone before, even the

Roman Catholic Bible, and the excellencies of all versions were incorporated into this great one. Never before had such labor and care been expended on the English Bible."

(6) The Revised version. "About the beginning of the nineteenth century, the appearance of several partial revisions, by private individuals, indicated the feeling in the minds of scholars that the time for a new Bible revision was at hand. As years went on the feeling grew stronger. The discovery of the most ancient manuscripts, that were entirely unknown in King James' time, the changes in our language, and the defects even in the noble version itself, made a thorough revision necessary. This was undertaken by the Church of England, which formed two companies of distinguished scholars from all denominations, one for the Old Testament and one for the New, with corresponding American companies working in close co-operation. After ten and one-half years of labor, in 1881, the Revised New Testament was published, and after four years more, in 1885, the Revised Old Testament. In 1901 (having waited according to agreement) the American revisers published the American revision, containing their own preferences, so far as they had not been adopted by the English companies." (Wells.) The American Revision is undoubtedly the best translation of the Scriptures ever made. No Sunday-school teacher can afford to do his work without using this revision.

Topics for Class Discussion

1. What is a Bible manuscript?
2. Describe the library of an ancient church.
3. Name some of the lost manuscripts.
4. The three oldest manuscripts of the Bible in existence to-day.
5. John Wycliffe's version of the Bible.

Topics for Class Papers

1. The Sinaitic manuscript of the Bible.
2. The story of the English Bible.

LESSON IX

THE BIBLE AND JESUS THE CHRIST

Reference literature. Thompson, "Christ in the Old Testament"; Conley, "The Bible in Modern Light," Chap. XIV; Mathews, "Messianic Hope in the New Testament"; Hovey, "The Bible," Chap. IV; Geistweit, "The Young Christian and His Bible," Chaps. X and XI.

1. *Jesus the Christ is the heart of the Bible.* The name "the Christ" and "the Messiah" mean the same thing in the Bible—both meaning the Anointed One. Now this "Anointed One" or "Jesus the Christ" is the heart of the Bible. In the Old Testament it is Christ to come; in the New Testament it is Christ already come and to come again. The work of the Christ or the Messiah is always *to deliver.* In the Old Testament he is the one through whom Jehovah will deliver his people from their sins and from the oppression of the nations. From "the first gospel" in Gen. 3 : 15 on through type and prophecy, sacrifice and symbol, story and history, this Messianic hope is ever at hand. In the New Testament he it is who will deliver not only Israel but all nations and peoples that put their trust in him from sin and eternal death. It is the person and work of Jesus the Christ in the Bible that gives that book supreme power over the hearts of men. The authority of the Bible is first and last the authority of the Christ within it. Take him out of it, and it will be as powerless as the preaching of the Talmud.

2. *The Old Testament is the product of the Messianic hope of Israel.* To say this is to say that Christ made the Old Testament, and this is true. If there had been no

Messiah to come there would have been no Old Testament as we have it, for the Old Testament is preeminently a book of prophecy. "It breathes a spirit of hope and expectancy. This does not necessarily refer to sayings that were prophetic, but rather to the spirit that possessed the writers and characterized the material they produced. There is the outworking of a purpose that ever looks to a great final revelation of something—to a condition of life that should be perfect, an ideal humanity, in which righteousness and peace should reign and God and man shall be in harmony. Isa. 35 expresses the hope of the ages. This prophetic spirit produces two visions: a Person, and a kingdom. From the very beginning there was held out the hope of a coming One who should be a deliverer. The history of the Old Testament is also prophetic. That is, it is never a completed history. While this may be said of all history it is yet particularly true of history in the Old Testament. It is ever looking forward to something better, something permanent. God is moving in that history in a peculiar way. This prophetic history becomes more apparent as we follow the story of Moses. He is simply a passing leader; he tells of another who is to come. Moses is succeeded by Joshua. The judges cross the pages in what seems to the reader a rapid succession. The kings come and go. But through all these changes the hope that better things are in store is not allowed to perish, and when it would seem as though the national light must go out in darkness, the beacon of promise is lighted again by some prophet of the Lord, and the people lift their faces in its glow. Even after prophecy closed, as recorded in the Old Testament, this prophetic spirit is discovered in the apocryphal and apocalyptic literature." (Geistweit in "The Young Christian and His Bible," pp. 93-95.) From all this it is clear that the Old Testament as a whole is due to the coming One about whom it tells.

3. *The Messianic life and work of Jesus fulfils the Messianic hope and prophecy of the Old Testament.* To the two disciples on the way to Emmaus, on the day of his resurrection, he himself said: "O foolish men and slow of heart to believe in all that the prophets have spoken. Behooved it not the Christ to suffer these things and to enter into his glory? And beginning from Moses and from all the prophets he interpreted to them in all the Scriptures the things concerning himself." This does not mean that the teachings of the Old Testament prophets did not have an immediate application in their day. The historical study of the Bible is helping us to see more and more the message of the prophets to the people of their own times. But there is also the element of larger and more remote fulfilment, in which the purposes of God for the whole world can be seen and understood. This larger element in the Old Testament Jesus fulfilled, or is fulfilling as the days of the kingdom come and go. He himself said that "one jot or one tittle shall in nowise pass away from the law till all things be accomplished." According to Micah, the Messiah was to be born in Bethlehem of Judea, and he was born there in the days of Cæsar Augustus. According to Isaiah he was to be Immanuel, and he was in truth the "Word made flesh." According to Gen. 3 : 15 he was to bruise the serpent's head, and in the wilderness temptation he gave that old enemy of the human race his death blow, and saw him fall as lightning from his high place. The outlines of the Messiah's character in the Old Testament Jesus lived out and wrought out in their essential elements. The picture of the "suffering Servant of Jehovah" there drawn, he more than fulfilled. The hope of deliverance that runs through both history and prophecy he has been fulfilling for nineteen centuries.

4. *The New Testament is the outgrowth of this Messianic life and work of Jesus.* In fulfilling the Old Testament

Jesus created the materials for the New. He wrote no book himself, but his disciples and apostles in writing the story of his life, his teachings, his work, and his church gave us the book we call the New Testament. More than this, they wrote it under the influence of that Spirit which he sent to guide them into all truth, and to bring to their remembrance the things which he had said unto them. Thus the Old Testament and the New Testament are indissolubly joined together.

The gospel narratives tell the story of his life and work from several points of view. The book of Acts sketches for us the spread of his gospel of salvation and the organization of his disciples into churches, first among the Jews and then among the Gentiles. The epistles interpret for us the meaning of his message and his work as it is applied to the lives of sinful men and used by the Holy Spirit in their salvation and sanctification. The book of Revelation pictures the triumph of his truth and of his coming again to restore redeemed man to the eternal privileges of the "tree of life." Thus there will be ushered in through his work the new Eden—"the New Jerusalem which cometh down from God." What is lost in the Old Testament is regained in the New through the person and work of Jesus the Christ. In him the two books are joined together. Neither is perfect without the other, and neither can be understood without the other. All that is essential in the Old finds its fulfilment in the life and work of Jesus in the New. Hence, the New Testament, which is the story and the interpretation of that life and work for man is to us the book of all books for religion to-day. If we would know him and the power of his message we must turn to its pages day unto day. Through his words in that book he is ever speaking to man, for "they are spirit and they are life." It is here we find the ultimate ground for our prayerful and diligent study of the Bible.

As he said, we should search the Scriptures because they testify of him.

5. *The biblical conception of the person of Jesus.* The biblical conception of the person of Jesus the Messiah is a growing conception. It is a long way from the foregleam of a coming deliverer in Gen. 3 : 15, to the Logos doctrine of John in his Gospel. In the Old Testament there is first the idea of a coming deliverer, then of a prophet like unto Moses, then a distinct personality—the Anointed One, the Messiah, ordained of God to deliver Israel from all enemies and to set up a world kingdom, which would be universal and everlasting. This Messiah was thus to be the son of David. Further, he came to be thought of in the mind of the prophet as Immanuel, that is God with us. To an extent therefore he was to be in the place of Jehovah to the chosen people. Last of all he was to be the "suffering Servant of Jehovah" in this work of deliverance, though the mass of the Jews never dreamed of a Messiah as suffering in the work which was given him to do. Rather he could slay the nations with the breath of his mouth, and make the enemies of Israel lick the dust. The question of the divinity, or deity, of the Messiah was never thought of perhaps by the Jews. The Son of man was indeed to be a unique being, but he was never identified in personal essence with Jehovah.

In the New Testament the gospel narratives indicate that the disciples first thought of Jesus as the Messiah come to earth. Their conception of him grew as they went with him from day to day, but they never got away from the thought that he was a human personality, and that he would set up an earthly kingdom, till after the descent of the Spirit on the day of Pentecost. Even Peter's confession that Jesus was the Son of God can hardly be construed to mean that Peter identified Jesus in personal being with God. But during the life of Jesus "the presence of something more than human made itself felt. Those who watched him asked, 'What manner of man is this?' 'Who is this that forgiveth sins also?' Human though he was no other human being was like him. After his death came the divine surprise of his resurrection, then his ascension, then the day of Pentecost. On that day his friends recognized Jesus as exalted at the right hand of God, and exerting divine power upon men. His disciples called upon his name or prayed to him. The first martyr died with 'Lord Jesus, receive my spirit' upon his lips. In the experience of Paul a transforming spiritual power which he recognized as the power of Jesus flashed forth victoriously, and Paul thenceforth knew him as a divine Saviour. Jesus was no second God to these disciples: they felt that to pray to him was not different from praying to the God of their fathers. Their simple faith and straightforward love found him more than human, and it came to pass that they adored him with God, and God by means of him."

It is not strange that we find the New Testament writers teaching his divinity in their books and letters. That Matthew and Luke believed in his divinity is seen from the story of his birth as narrated in the infancy sections of these two Gospels. Paul unquestionably teaches the divinity and preexistence of Jesus. John in his Logos doctrine identifies Jesus with God from the beginning. But the teaching of the divinity of Jesus by the writers of the New Testament not only grew out of their religious experience of the Christ within, but out of the teaching of Jesus himself. If we make a careful study of the self-consciousness of Jesus as portrayed in his teaching we come to see that he thought of himself as being in a very unique sense in vital union with God. Indeed in the Johannine representation of that teaching, he declared himself to be one with the Father. The nature of this oneness is certainly far above any unity that man sustains to God, but of the nature of this union as to the essence we can never know. It is beyond our experience and it is nowhere revealed to us in the New Testament.

Topics for Class Discussion

1. The prophetic spirit in the Old Testament.
2. Jesus and the Messianic hope of the Old Testament.
3. How far does Jesus fulfil this Messianic hope?
4. Wherein is the New Testament the outgrowth of the life and the work of Jesus?
5. What gives the Bible such captivating authority in the lives of men?

Topics for Class Papers

1. How Jesus made the Bible.
2. The Bible doctrine of the person of Jesus.

LESSON X

METHODS OF BIBLE STUDY

Prof. E. B. Pollard, PH. D.

Reference literature. Griffith-Thomas, " Methods of Bible Study "; Broadus and others, " Hints on Bible Study "; Sell, " Bible Study by Books "; Lee, " Bible Study Popularized "; Hazard-Fowler, " The Books of the Bible "; Moulton, " The Literary Study of the Bible."

The need of a method in Bible study. The Bible is like the rich soil in the plains of Palestine, which yielded abundant harvests, notwithstanding the crude stick plows with which the Oriental farmer merely scratched the surface of the ground. The Scriptures will give up a wealth of helpfulness to the honest student, whatever may be his method. And yet one should not be satisfied with a spiritual yield which merely keeps one from starvation, when better methods might bring richer harvests for himself, and also enough to dispense to others for their growth. While the methods of studying the Bible are many, we here call attention to but five, each of which has its own advantages, and no one of them is in itself sufficient for the making of an all-round Bible student and teacher. All five must be employed, more or less, for the best acquaintance with the Book of books.

I. *The first may be called the literary and historical method.* Here is kept constantly in the foreground two well-known facts—that this revelation from God has come to us in the form of a written message, that is, *literature,* and also that the deeds and thoughts recorded have an *historical* relation to the periods with which they deal, or out of which, humanly speaking, they had their rise. So we have in the Bible early as well as later, poetry and song; history based upon earlier documents and reliable tradition, as well as the statements of contemporary annalists; prophecy from various periods and crises in the life of Israel; wisdom from earlier and later sages; gospels of Jesus Christ; history of apostolic labors; letters to individuals and to churches, and Apocalypse—all these thoroughly interwoven with the actual life of mankind upon the globe. The Bible is preeminently a book of life, *the* book of life; and since life generally has found its best and most enduring expression in literature, it is not strange that this means should have been chosen as the vehicle for the divine revelation to the world. The advantage of this first method of study, therefore, is that it discloses the real *humanity* of the book; and proves the Bible all the more divine, because so supremely and deeply human.

This method of study may be briefly illustrated by an example. The book of Ruth has been chosen for study. Let it be read in its entirety, first for the simple and beautiful story which it tells. Then, a more careful study of its features will disclose that it is a most engaging idyllic prose poem; parts of it rising to the heights of pure Hebrew poetry with its balancing of line against line in complete parallelism. Romance follows tragedy. The struggle to "keep the wolf from the door" in days of famine; love, marriage, death, widowhood follow in rapid succession. Embers of a latent patriotism and religious fealty burn bright again; motherly solicitude and filial piety shine forth as if to vie with each other in brilliant loyalty. A maidenlike coyness and a maternal intrigue; a love at first sight and a happy fruitful marriage—all these go into the making of this divinely inspired pastoral.

Read again and carefully study the historical setting of the book. Find its niche in the life of God's chosen people. It was "in the days when the judges ruled." See Moab, destined to play no unimportant part in later history; and the famine, which not uncommon, again and again played a providential rôle in the shaping of human destinies; the intermarriage with heathen people, not so strictly under the ban as at a later period; Oriental customs and Hebrew laws of the harvest; laws of consanguinity and inheritance; the levirate marriage; the custom of "the loosed shoe"; Ruth as ancestress of David and so of the Messiah.

Such a study would be literary and historical and of much interest and value. But it is to be remembered that this method deals with the outward form and circumstances of the revelation not with the substance; the vehicle, not the life; the body, not the soul which animates and give the book its significant value. And yet since the body is the soul's interpreter, so no one should neglect to study the form of the revelation, that this may aid to a clearer knowledge of the soul within.

2. *A second method of Bible study may be called the critical, or the more intensive, method.* With the very best available text of the inspired word before us, our object is to get the exact meaning of the writer. We are greatly indebted to patient scholars who have carefully compared the old manuscripts and the ancient versions and quotations from early Christian writers, in order to give us as nearly as possible the original words of inspired prophet and apostle; to those who have studied zealously the ancient languages and brought to all the meaning of the Scripture writers in plain speech of to-day. By their help we all can do a little critical study for ourselves. The critical process may be exegetical, and it may be analytical. For not only must the meaning of words be carefully studied with lexicon and grammar, but their relation to the context and to the entire writing. So also the language, the literary style of the writing may be care-

fully examined. Such questions may be answered as: Who was the author? When did he live? Under what circumstances did he write? To whom and why? Is the book from one writer or from more than one? Is it a single discourse or a collection of discourses written or delivered at different times? Does the writer give evidence of being an eye-witness of what he records? Does he make use of historical and literary material of those who had preceded him? Does external evidence—facts from other books or other sources—throw any light upon the evidence which the study of the book itself discloses?

Such a study is largely intellectual and technical in character; its chief purpose being to understand the exact meaning of the Scripture and to find the proper place of its parts in the plan and progress of the ever-unfolding revelation of God. The student should therefore make use of the best critical helps, expositions, and commentaries which are available, always remembering, however, that the Scriptures can never be fully appreciated by studying words, nor analyzing documents.

3. We shall next notice the third method of study. As the one just described may be termed intensive, this is more *ex*tensive. It is study by books. While the methods already mentioned also proceed with study by books, yet the point of view, purpose, and so the method are different. Here the aim is primarily to get at the real message of a book as a whole. It is one of the sanest and most valuable of all methods. It proceeds upon the assumption that each particular writing had its own spiritual purpose and was framed in accordance with that design. It undertakes to get at the heart of each writer; to know what was the mind of the Spirit in moving the author to his task. Hence, a particular sentence, section, or chapter is not studied without reference to the intent and teaching of that of which these are but parts. The book is treated as

a living whole. The context is recognized as a part of the text, as the text of the context. Thus the Scriptures are not seen as a patchwork of precepts, or as an arsenal of proof-texts, but as living messages of vital power and comprehensive meaning. Even so complete a gem as that of Paul on love, in 1 Cor. 13, has a far richer value when we study it in the light of the purpose and message of the entire Epistle to the church at Corinth. The Gospel of Matthew must be understood in the light of its design as a whole—to show to the Jewish mind that Jesus of Nazareth fulfilled the requirements of the promised Old Testament Messiah.

From this it may be seen how valuable is the exercise of making an entire book and its message the unit of study.

4. *The topical method.* One's purpose may be to discover the biblical teaching upon a single subject, a single doctrine, or upon a single character. Or the aim may be to find the teaching of a particular prophet or apostle upon a single truth; or to study Christ's teaching upon a definite theme. What is technically called biblical theology has in recent years made more prominent this method of study. For example, one may wish to know the teaching of Jesus on the subject of the "kingdom of God" as given by the evangelists; or to study Paul's doctrine of the "atonement." All the Gospels, or all of Paul's Epistles, would be studied for the light that may be thrown by them upon these respective problems. The soul-winning teacher may study to bring together and master those passages of Scripture which answer the question "How may one be saved?" the nature of sin; the natural condition of the human heart; the need of a Saviour; the duty of repentance and of faith. In this way a comprehensive view may be had of great Scripture truths and doctrines.

This, remember, is quite different from the vicious habit which may be called "the concordance method" by which one finds out how many times a certain word is used in the Bible, and then throwing these indiscriminately together, without regard to their real meaning in the several passages, concludes that he has the biblical teaching on a particular subject. This kind of treatment is subversive of all accurate and sane Bible study and is to be shunned.

5. *Next we have the devotional method of studying the Bible.* Here the purpose is not intellectual, but preeminently spiritual, and the method that of heartsearching meditation. It is communing with the truth; surrendering the heart to the Spirit that he may guide the reader into the very light into which he led the inspired writer at the first. Here the soul gives itself up to the sensitizing power of the Holy Spirit, and bathes itself in the warmth and glow of heavenly light. This is not to say that in the use of all the foregoing methods the guidance of the Spirit may not be, and should not be, sought. He was given to guide us into all the truth, and his help must be sought for the best results in them all. But here preeminently we have a spiritual exercise. The student here reads and lets the truth permeate to his own inner soul. He goes over it, yielding to it, till he "knows it by heart." Here one finds the atmosphere through which the truth discovered by the other methods is disclosed in its truest light. Here sight becomes vision; the ear hears the fainter whisperings, the voice of gentle stillness. Here the soul-hunger is satisfied by the heavenly manna. Here the heart opens to receive the fulness, which as a new-filled reservoir refreshes the life and gives it driving power to dare and to do, causing one to exclaim with the psalmist

> O, how I love thy law
> It is my meditation all the day.

Finally, the true Bible study, the comprehensive, the adequate Bible study will be a combination of all these methods. The first two deal primarily with the form, the other three with the content of revelation; the former with the body of it, the latter with its soul. The literary and historical study is interested with the body as the artist with the human form; the critical study with the form as the anatomist with the human frame. These are legitmate and necessary. But how little, after all, we should know of the meaning of man's life in the world if we stopped with a study of the cells of the brain, the muscles and bones, or even with the artist's portrayal of form. The mind and soul must be known. This too is true of the Book. Its heart treasures must be fathomed; its spiritual effluence felt, or Bible teaching will lack the true dynamic; that the man of God may be complete, thoroughly furnished unto every good work.

Topics for Class Discussion

1. The Bible to be studied as any other book—yes and no.
2. Criticism—the lower; the higher. Constructive and destructive.
3. The Bible in modern English literature and oratory.
4. Biblical helps that have helped me. Helps that hinder.
5. The Bible as a soul winner's book.

Topics for Class Papers

1. The historical study of the Bible.
2. The time and place of the devotional study of the Bible.

Part II

The Great Vital Doctrines of the Bible

"And ye shall know the truth and the truth shall make you free" (John 8 : 32).

"Thy word is truth" (John 17 : 17).

LESSON I

GOD

Reference literature. Strong, "Systematic Theology," Vol. I; Clarke, "Outlines of Christian Theology," Part I; Hovey, "Christian Doctrine and Life"; Geistweit, "The Young Christian and His Bible"; Bushnell, "God in Christ"; Westcott, "Revelation of the Father"; Robertson, "The Teaching of Jesus concerning God the Father"; Abbott, "The Personality of God"; Bowne, "Immanence of God."

1. *There is a God.* The Bible begins with God. Its first words are: "In the beginning God." This is its first message—*God is.* It nowhere undertakes to prove the existence of God. To the biblical writers there is no need of this, for the heavens declare that fact. "Their line has gone out throughout all the earth, and their words to the end of the world" proclaiming not only the existence of God but his glory. The burden of proof is with the one who would deny this. Only the fool hath said in his heart, "There is no God." What nature so well declares the Bible writers know also from their personal religious experience and from divine revelations given to them. To pause to prove the existence of God would be to them waste of time.

2. *The being of God.* Man has ever sought to know God. "Upon the conception that is entertained of God will depend the nature and quality of his religion." The universe about man helps him to learn something about the nature of God, but not enough to satisfy the hunger of his soul after God. The Bible with its superior revelation comes to his relief in this matter. It reveals to him something of what God is in his essential nature. In the person of the

Christ in the Bible we get our highest conception of God. He is the "express image of the Father's person."

(1) First of all God is a spirit. The word "spirit" refers to the essence, or being, of God. "When Christ said 'God is a spirit' he doubtless implied that God is immaterial; but that was not his main thought, and what he affirmed was something far more positive and valuable. What is a spirit? How do we know? We know through our own consciousness. Man has a body but is a spirit, and is conscious of himself as a spirit—that is, as a being who thinks and feels and wills. These are the essential powers of a spirit, and it is from our own possession of these powers that we know what it means that God is a spirit. It means that God is an intelligence; God is a mind. He thinks and feels and wills." (Clarke.)

(2) God as a spiritual being is personal. Personality is implied in the word spirit, as used above. God is not a power or force or law. A law cannot think or feel or will. The word "personal" asserts self-consciousness and self-direction in God; for these are the powers of personality as it is known to man. "A personal spirit is a self-conscious and self-directing intelligence; and a personal God is a God who knows himself as himself and consciously directs his own actions." He ever reveals himself as "I" and man in his clearest moments of thought addresses him as "Thou."

(3) God as a personal spirit is infinite. "God is infinite, not as being immeasurably vast and extended in space, but as being free from all such limitations as we find upon all our powers and activities. Our powers reach their limits, his never. In this high sense he is infinite in all his attributes. Every quality in him exists unhindered and to the full, so that in every department of his activity to him all things are possible." (Clarke.) God is infinite in time. "Before the mountains were brought forth or ever thou

hadst formed the world, even from everlasting to everlasting, thou art God" (Ps. 90 : 2). Thus God is self-existent. He is also infinite in power. The omnipotence of God is seen in his creation and in his government of the world, and also in the salvation of man through the person and work of Jesus Christ his only begotten Son. Again, God is infinite in knowledge. He sees the end from the beginning. Nothing is therefore hid from his intelligence. Futhermore he is unlimited in his presence. While his personality is above man and the world, which he created, yet he is immanent in both. His spirit is omnipresent. "Whither shall I go from thy spirit, or whither shall I flee from thy presence? If I ascend into heaven, thou art there; if I make my bed in hell, behold thou art there. If I take the wings of the morning and dwell in the uttermost parts of the sea; even there shall thy hand lead me, and thy right hand shall hold me" (Ps. 139 : 7-10).

(4) God is not only personal but is tri-personal. "The doctrine of tri-personality rests upon the testimony of the Scriptures, a testimony which, so far as the New Testament is concerned, is as clear as that for the unity of God; for Christ speaks to the Father and of the Father, habitually, as another person; he also speaks of the Holy Spirit as another Comforter, in distinction from himself, the designation being therefore clearly personal. Yet he claims to be one with the Father in power and operation. The two doctrines are by no means contradictory, for the triplicity is clearly personal, while the unity may well be essential. Moreover, unity of spiritual essence, with all that it involves of sameness in knowledge, feeling, and will, must render the personal distinctions of the Godhead very slight in effect, as compared with personal distinctions between man and man." (Hovey.)

3. *The characteristics or attributes of God.* We have seen that God, according to the Christian conception, is a

personal spirit. Now this personal spiritual being is characterized by certain moral qualities or attributes. "The attributes of God are those distinguishing characteristics of a divine nature which are inseparable from the idea of God and which constitute the basis and ground for his various manifestations to his creatures." (Strong.)

(1) "Love is the central attribute of God. The other moral attributes are but the same attribute seen from various limited points of view. The natural attributes describe the infinite resources at the disposal of infinite love. These resources love needs for its full manifestation. In God we have infinite love armed with infinite wisdom and power. This conception of God is the loftiest and most attractive known to man." ("A Manual of Theology," Beet, p. 82.)

(2) God is "perfectly good." "Be ye therefore perfect even as your Father which is in heaven is perfect" (Matt. 5 : 48). "The definition 'perfectly good' attributes to God all possible moral excellence. It declares him good without qualification, in the sense that the word bears at its best in the language of men. The conception of God as perfectly good is the crowning characteristic of Christian revelation, and to that revelation we are mainly indebted for it. Evidence of his goodness has been sought in nature, and found in part. But in Christ God has been expressed in life and action, and been shown as the good God, excellent in all respects, and worthy of the love and confidence of all beings." (Clarke.) The desire of God for the well-being of his creatures is an expression of his goodness. The grace of God in forgiving sinners is his goodness as exercised toward the guilty. The mercy of God is his goodness toward those who are miserable as well as guilty. And the patience and long-suffering of God is his goodness as exercised in forbearing to punish at once the sinful.

(3) God is holy. The holiness of God is more than his goodness. "By holiness is meant the moral purity and recitude of the divine Being." (Hovey.) God is righteous in all his acts as well as in his being. "He cannot contradict himself, but is morally capable only of action that truly expresses his character. His inner perfection is the sole inspiration and standard of his conduct. He acts in perfect freedom; and every act of his perfect freedom is in perfect harmony with his perfect character." God is thus the source and standard of right for man. His will as the expression of his holy nature is our law of conduct. What he acts upon he requires us to act upon.

(4) God is just. "God's holiness dictates the end for which he creates and is conducting the universe. He can have no ultimate end, as a being of perfect goodness, except to produce goodness. Since holiness dictates God's end in the universe, it follows that for all beings who are capable of goodness, holiness, or strong and consistent goodness, is necessarily the standard. This he requires. He cannot have one standard for himself and another for his creatures; hence he requires men to be holy, and endeavors to make them so." (Clarke.) Thus he is always just. The justice of God is his holiness as thus exercised in moral government, in legislation, retribution, etc. "Justice in God, as the revelation of his holiness, is devoid of all passion or caprice. There is in God no selfish anger. The penalties he inflicts upon transgression are not vindictive but vindicative. They express the revulsion of God's nature from moral evil, the judicial indignation of purity against impurity, the self-assertion of infinite holiness against its antagonist and would-be destroyer." (Strong.)

4. *The relation of God to the universe and to man.* God as a personal spirit is characterized by modes of activity. He is not a far-away static God, but is an ever-present,

living, and working God. Jesus said, "My Father worketh hitherto." "Through the whole course of revelation God appears as a being far more full of life than any that he has created; his thought is creative, his feeling is intense, his action is infinitely free and powerful. This conception of the Living God, with the accompanying sense of his reality, presence, and power, is essential to all vital religion." (Clarke.)

(1) God is the creator of all things. "In the beginning God created the heavens and the earth" (Gen. 1 : 1). Then follows the story of this creation in detail including man. Whatever may have been the method of creation, the Scriptures affirm, not only in the great creation passages, but everywhere, that God is the source and creator of all. "The assertion is that the good personal Spirit lies back of the universe as the ground of its being, and the active cause of its existence. He brought it into being, and it owes itself to him. Plainly then he must be greater than the universe if he produced it. God dwells in the universe, and is active in the whole of it, but is not to be conceived as wholly occupied by it, or exhausting his possibilities in conducting its processes." (Clarke.)

(2) God is the sovereign ruler of all things. This government of God has respect to certain worthy ends. It is full of purpose. Not even a sparrow falls to the ground without the Father's notice. This government is also supreme. It embraces the whole universe. "In some sense, therefore, every act and event, great or small, is embraced in the plan of his government." "Again, this government exercises a control which is immediate as well as mediate; and physical as well as moral. By immediate control must be understood an exercise of divine power directly upon an object. Thus if the Spirit of God, having access to the spirit of man, touches it directly in the act of regeneration, the influence is properly called immediate. By mediate

control is meant divine power transmitted through one object, or more than one, to something else in which a change is wrought. By physical control is meant, control exercised by the use of material forces or media. Moral control is exercised by means of truth, by appealing to the reason and conscience, the hopes and fears, the sensibilities and desires of personal beings. It is in some respects the highest form of control." (Hovey.)

(3) God exercises a fatherly love toward his creations. He saw all that he had made, and it seemed good, or pleasing to him. The Bible from beginning to end speaks of this attitude of God, especially toward man. But in the person of Jesus, as the great revealer of God to men, this fatherly love finds its fulness of expression. God's attitude toward the universe is not only that of creator and ruler but of servant and father. "The universal sovereign is the universal servant, and if he cease to serve the universe would cease to be." In relation to man God is the loving father seeking to preserve and save men under the highest goodness. "Faithfully does he intend the good of that which he has created, and faithfully does he seek it. If his creatures are responsive and obedient, his helpful and educative care is ever with them to lead them to their destiny of likeness to himself. If they are disobedient, and so misuse his gift of freedom as to practise moral evil, which he hates, still he unchangingly holds toward them the attitude of a true father."

(4) God is the redeemer of man. We have seen that the holiness of God points out that the ends of the universe must be spiritual. "In the Christian life we safely affirm that the purpose of God in creating and conducting the universe is first to produce free spirits, capable of goodness like unto his own, and then to bring them into his own moral likeness and fellowship." So far as this relates to man sin has run across this holy purpose of God

and broken up the fellowship. Yet God because of his fatherly attitude toward man loves the sinner and is ever seeking to save that which has been lost. He is thus the redeemer of sinning mankind. In this redemption God works along many lines. In giving to man moral law, and in requiring of man strict conformity to that law, he leads man to a sense of his utter sinfulness. In permitting the consequences of man's sin to be visited upon him he causes him to cry out for deliverance. To all who repent of their sin and cry out for this deliverance God is their everlasting redeemer. This redemption is through the anointed Messiah of God, who is the Lamb slain from the foundation of the world. That man might see God's willingness to redeem, and the way of redemption, he sent this anointed Messiah, his only begotten Son, into the world. Thus in Jesus Christ we see God as our redeemer.

Topics for Class Discussion

1. Why the Bible does not prove the existence of God.
2. The being of God.
3. The inherent characteristics of God.
4. Justice and the love of God.
5. How we may know God.

Topics for Class Papers

1. The personality of God.
2. The relation of God to the universe and to man.

LESSON II

SIN AND ITS CONSEQUENCES

Rev. J. Milnor Wilbur

Reference literature. Clarke, " Outline of Christian Theology," Part III; Stevens, " Teachings of Jesus," Chap. IX; Conley, " Evolution of Man "; Orr, " God's Image in Man," Chap. V; Geistweit, " The Young Christian and His Bible "; Hovey, " The Bible," pp. 134-139, 171-173.

1. *Sin is a universal fact and a universal experience.* No race of people has yet been found that did not have some sense of sin; it is not always well defined; it may be only a sense of loss or of suffering, but in every human breast there is a consciousness of wrong-doing. The Bible does not try to prove that men are sinners, it takes it for granted and addresses human beings as sinners. Other religions do the same, though with a modified meaning of sin. Every man has a conscience, and so what is thus recognized in religions is a consciousness of sin with every man. That sense of wrong-doing may be more keen in some than in others, conscience may be more sensitive in some than in others, but all men recognize themselves when addressed as sinners. The man who does not know he has done wrong is the man who hasn't all his faculties.

2. *Three explanations of sin:* (1) Man has a body; he is thus allied to the brute, and whatever there is of wrong-doing in him is due to this animalism. Get rid of the body and you get rid of sin. This makes the body in itself evil; accounts only for sins that have to do with the flesh. (2) Man is growing, he is not full-grown, and sin is a part of his education into something better. The child sticks his

linger in the fire in order to learn not to do it; we must do wrong in order to learn not to do wrong. This takes away blame, and relieves a man of all responsibility. It contradicts a man's consciousness of blameworthiness. It is also contrary to man's experience, for doing wrong does not always or generally teach man to shun evil but on the other hand often gives him a love for it. (3) The word most frequently used in the Bible, translated "sin," is the word that means "failure" or "missing the mark." What is that mark that man has missed? It is the chief end for which he was created: to give honor to God. We are God's creatures, brought into the world in love and for our interests, with the special privilege of becoming like him, and of associating with him. In so far as we do wrong this becomes to us impossible and to God painful. We are created with a divine likeness, with a spiritual constitution like God; when we sin, instead of using this godlike constitution for the building of a good character, we pervert it and build a selfish one; instead of using it for virtue and goodness we use it for vice and badness. Our nature was made for and aimed at the high and the right; we have "missed the mark" by hitting the low and the wrong. Our wills were made to be parallel with God's will and so bring about a likeness in character to God; we have used our wills for our own selfish purposes and missed the character that we might have had.

3. *Sin has its seat not in our flesh nor in our environment, but in our wills.* No man has to sin; it is his choice when he does sin. The love of God is the supreme law of life; when we fail thus to put God in his natural relation to us we are putting our wills up against God's; it is displacing God from his rightful place by putting ourselves in that place. It is a choice of self instead of God; we become wil-ful instead of will-ing children. Sin is bad and condemnatory because it is man's preference. If it

is a sin of the body it is because we prefer the animal. If it is a sin of the circumstances in which we are placed it is because we prefer yielding. We all indeed have a natural or inherited bias to sin which influences our will, but we have also the assurance of divine help to enable us to make right choices and live right lives. It may then be justly said that man's actions are determined by his own free choice, or will, and that when he does wrong he is deliberately bringing his higher nature under his lower and using his will for ends and purposes for which he was not created. We can verify this idea of sin by asking in what did the sinlessness of Jesus consist? While divine he was also a man, yet without sin. He was capable of sinning because he was capable of being tempted. He had the endowments of the ordinary man and began life with the same advantages and the same disadvantages; his bodily appetites, his undeveloped life—for he grew—were identical with the race to which he belonged. He was subjected to every constraint and limitation of mankind. Why didn't he sin? Simply because he didn't want to, because he didn't choose to. His choice was to do his Father's will; he willed not to do his own will, and because he asserted his will in the direction of the purpose for which he was sent into the world, and for which every other man is created, there was no unrighteousness in him. Though tempted in all points like we are he was yet without sin, because he chose to give his Father his rightful place in his life. The sinlessness of Jesus was, therefore, because he chose to live a life in conformity with his Father's will. "Our wills are ours, we know not how, our wills are ours to make them thine." The man who fails to do that is the sinner.

4. *Two consequences follow man's act of sinning:* (1) It brings sorrow to God. "I will tell you of my life-sorrow when I see you," wrote a friend some time ago. God has a life-sorrow; he has a thorn in his heart's happiness: it is

man's preference for himself above God, his choice of wrong instead of right. The one who suffers most when the man goes wrong is God; the terrible biting of an awakened conscience cannot compare with the agony in his heart when one of his children goes astray. The only conception we can get of it is the cost it must have been to God to give up his only begotten Son. The suffering Christ is only a faint disclosure of the pain of the God who sent him. It was time for the sun to be darkened and the moon to refuse to give her light when man who was created to be God's chief glory so perverted his life as to become God's chief sorrow. We do well to pause before doing a deed that will bring tears to the heart of so loving a God. (2) The other consequence is that through sin man is lost. A thing is lost when it is not in its right place; man is lost because he has gotten away from where he belonged. He has debased his likeness to God and put it where it does not belong; he has used it for ends for which it was not made. The innocency with which he was created is no longer his, and the character for which God gave him the possibility has not been attained; he is away from his rightful place in God's plan. He is lost to the purposes for which God created him, lost to the true expression of his right relation to God, lost to the true aim of man's immortal being. Jesus considered that man belonged to God and we are to judge whether a soul is lost or not by the attitude it sustains to God. The prodigal son was lost the moment his proper attitude toward his father was changed.

5. *This lost condition, if not altered, becomes the saddest condition in which one can find himself, and the most intolerable.* The word " depart" tells an awful story: it means that that nature which was fitted for association with God has, by its sinning, so disqualified itself for that association as now to be deprived of fellowship with God. The man who chooses to live for himself must finally live

alone with himself. He becomes unprofitable, good-for-nothing, and must take his place with the drift and refuse of the universe. His relation to God becomes completely changed; God can no longer look upon him with favor; he is opposed to God and God cannot regard him as anything other than he is. He has missed the mark, he has failed of God's intent, he has placed his own selfish and temporary interests above God, he has courted by this action the disfavor of God; he thus becomes by the law of his own being condemned to suffer the consequences. It is impossible to define or even suggest all the ultimate consequences of sin. Sometimes it is remorse, the sting of conscience—and what worse suffering than to be pursued day in and day out by a guilty conscience? Sometimes it is bodily suffering; sometimes it is the gradual loss of capacity for the good and the pure and the right, the loss of the sense of right and wrong, absolute moral degeneracy. The worst thing that sin does for us is to make it next to impossible to get rid of it; to be conscious of sin and not able to get rid of it is the most intolerable condition conceivable. To know that a habit is wrong, to recognize that it is doing us harm, and to realize that it is making God's heart ache, yet owing to the prolonged indulgence in that habit to have become so weak-willed as not to be able to throw it off, is to be of all men most miserable; it is being lashed with our own thoughts, chastised with our own emotions, scourged with the pursuing love of the heavenly Father whom we are constantly conscious of having wronged and grieved. Since life continues into the future, if sin remains the decisive element in its choices, we can expect nothing else than that the same consequences continue: eternal sin will be followed by eternal consequences. "These shall go away into everlasting punishment." This departure is the result of their own choice. Man reaps what he sows.

Topics for Class Discussion

1. The fall of man.
2. Why is sin universal?
3. Different views of sin.
4. The unpardonable sin.
5. The consequences for sin here and hereafter.

Topics for Class Papers

1. Evolution and the doctrine of the fall.
2. The first and worst sin.

LESSON III

DELIVERANCE FROM SIN THROUGH JESUS THE CHRIST

Rev. J. Milnor Wilbur

Reference literature. Griffith-Jones, "Ascent Through Christ"; Orr, "God's Image in Man," Chap. VI; Denny, "The Death of Christ"; Clarke, "Outline of Christian Theology," pp. 305-367; Van Dyke, "The Gospel for an Age of Sin"; Stevens, "The Teaching of Jesus," Chap. XII.

1. *As the experience of sin is universal the desire to get rid of it is also universal.* Paul's question "Who shall deliver me from this body that is dragging me to death?" is echoed in every life; the schemes and contrivances of the ethnic religions to scare away and avoid the evil spirits is only another phase of the problem.

2. *What is salvation?* Christianity teaches that Jesus the Christ came into the world to save sinners. To save sinners from what? What is salvation? (1) It is not simply bringing them to a place of safety; it is no such mechanical thing as "getting to heaven" if by that is meant the taking from one place and putting into another. Salvation is not a change of climate or environment. (2) Not taking away the penalty of wrong-doing. Many times it is impossible for salvation to take away the effects of sin. The reformed drunkard still wears his red nose and has to worry along with impaired faculties, and the thief has a hard time restoring confidence. God's grace and man's disgrace may go side by side. Jesus did not come to save us from hell so much as he did to save us from the sin which makes hell. To tell a man that he may steal and escape the penitentiary is not salvation; but to tell him how he may get over the

habit of stealing and the desire to steal, though he remain in the penitentiary, is salvation. A bad man in heaven would be still a bad man; a good man in hell would still be a good man.

3. *Two elements make up the salvation as given us in the Bible:* (1) Forgiveness. Jesus said at the Supper: "This is my blood of the new covenant shed for many for the remission of sins," and Paul speaks of Christ "in whom we have redemption, the forgiveness of sins." Forgiveness is God's willingness to treat a sinner as though he had never sinned; it does not change the fact of his sin nor can it always relieve man of the results of his wrong-doing, but it means that so far as God is concerned a man's wrong-doing will not be considered as affecting the relation between God and the man. Forgiveness puts sin away from between God and the man, and makes it as though sin had never been. This blots out the past and makes a man feel that he has another chance, a new beginning; there are no blots on the present page and there are no blots on the past page. (2) The second element is righteousness. "He died to make us good," the old hymn says. Paul says, "Conformed to the image of his Son" (Rom. 8 : 29). John's conception was that we should "be like him" (1 John 3 : 2). Jesus said he recognized as children of God, his brothers and sisters, only those who do the will of God (Matt. 12 : 50). This is not salvation by character but salvation into character; it is not getting a man into heaven but getting heaven into a man. People of opposite tendencies in character are not congenial; unless a man has some of the character, some of the moral likeness of Jesus Christ, he would find association with him a very uncongenial and uncomfortable thing. Our degree of happiness in heaven, as on earth, will be dependent upon the degree of likeness we bear in our characters to Jesus Christ. "Sow an act, reap a habit; sow a habit, reap a character; sow a character,

reap a destiny," said Doctor Boardman; and the kind of character we sow will determine the kind of destiny we reap. This is the meaning of "accounting for every idle word," "inasmuch as ye did it, or did it not," "work out your own salvation." Loss in opportunity means loss in character, and loss in character means loss in destiny. The heaven with all its happiness and glory, toward which we are looking and working, will be enjoyed in proportion to the capacity given us by our moral likeness to Jesus Christ. "Now is the day of salvation" because it is the day to receive God's forgiveness, and to begin the growing of our capacity for happiness which comes by fellowship with God.

4. *The mission of Jesus the Christ was to bring this salvation to men, to deliver them from sin past, present, and future.* (1) The first step in this deliverance is to get men to want to be delivered, so that Christ was God's judgment against sin in order to get man to see the heinousness of sin. He taught men as they had never been taught that sin is vile; the sense of evil burned itself into his very soul; from Bethlehem to Gethsemane, from Gethsemane to Calvary, the shame of sin forced itself upon him, and his whole nature revolted against it. He thus judged sin in order to achieve the sinner's salvation, by making him see sin as God sees it, and making his conscience hate it as God hates it. Jesus Christ did not make sin any more than the ray of light in the dark room makes the dust, but he made it known as it really is. The man who sees sin through the eyes of Jesus Christ must hate it. (2) It was not enough for the world to know the heinousness of sin; to know only that would be worse than despair. God meant the world not only to know about itself but about himself. We not only know sin through Christ but we know that he is our sin-bearer; he came to take the world's sin upon himself and to take it away from between God and man.

God would do his utmost to take men away from sin; only the Christ who bore the unique relation to the Father, could so fully exhibit God's readiness to forgive, and at the same time satisfy the demands of God's nature. He was willing to bear the sin of men, to identify himself with our sinful nature, and complete the sacrifice by dying for our sake and for God's sake. Christ is the sent of God; we know then that he satisfies every demand of God's nature in his effort after saving men; there is nothing more that can be done on God's part in order for a man to be saved. Whatever requirement there was in God that had to be met in his purpose to save men was met by Jesus Christ; there is no barrier on God's part. We may ask why Christ had to suffer and die? Why could he not be the triumphant Messiah instead of the suffering Messiah? Because nothing short of a complete life, lived to its fullest and emptied to its limit could meet the just demands of God or impress the heart of humanity. Spiritual slavery must be fought with spiritual weapons, and only suffering and death, the atoning death of the cross, could express God's self-sacrifice in bearing sin. Only thus could God disclose his hatred of sin and his love for the sinner. Our sins brought Christ to the cross, and only in the cross can we see redemption for human sin and the depth of divine love. Such a disclosure could be made in no other way than in the sacrifice of Jesus the Christ..

5. *Christ the pledge of this forgiveness and of help.* How may I know that I am forgiven and being saved? Because of the cross. The cross is the supreme assurance of salvation, sealing the covenant between God and man; Christ has pledged our acceptance with his blood. It also pledges his help for the future. We may come to see sin through the eyes of Christ and hate it as God hates it; we may come to see that Christ is our sin-bearer and has taken it away from between God and us; that is not enough:

yesterday and to-day are all right but how about to-morrow? Simply to show me what sin is and that it need not affect my relation to God if I am willing to forsake sin, without giving the ability to forsake it, is not salvation. In the old Anglo-Saxon Bible the word we have rendered Saviour is rendered Helper: "Born this day in the city of David, a Helper, which is Christ the Lord"; "Through Jesus Christ our Helper"; "The Father has sent the Son as Helper of the world." Either we need God or we do not; either he is able to help us or he is not; God's life is either communicable or it is not. The incarnation shows his life communicated to humanity. Pentecost assured men that God was still with them though they thought he had deserted them. Paul speaks of "knowing him and the power of his resurrection," his resurrection power, the power of his life coming into us as the result of his resurrection. Christ said: "Lo, I am with you always," and in the light of this we want to read Paul's statement in 1 Cor. 10 : 13. Then the question is not "What can I do?" but "What can God and I do?" The fact of Christ means that God's life is communicated to us as the power by which we may overcome evil, for "the Lord knoweth how to deliver the godly out of temptation." A life of true and vital righteousness is not an impossibility with such a Saviour.

Topics for Class Discussion

1. Why the sinner needs a Saviour.
2. Deliverance from sin in the Old Testament dispensation.
3. What is deliverance from sin—or salvation?
4. Man's efforts to free himself from sin.
5. Jesus the great and only Deliverer from sin.

Topics for Class Papers

1. The hunger of man to be delivered from sin.
2. Jesus, God's eternal and universal answer to the hunger.

LESSON IV

REPENTANCE AND FAITH THE CONDITIONS OF DELIVERANCE

Rev. J. Milnor Wilbur

Reference literature. Hyde, "God's Education of Man"; Clarke, "Outline of Christian Theology," pp. 395-409; Eaton, "Faith and the Faith"; Hall, "Relations of Faith and Life"; Jefferson, "Faith and Life"; Herrmann, "Faith and Morals"; Purves, "Faith and Life."

1. *Man's attitude.* When a man considers the great subject of his salvation, after finding out what Christ has done and is willing to do, he next wants to know what he must do. It is evident that Christ's attitude toward him is not the whole story: man must take some attitude toward Christ. The two words that Jesus used as expressing what he considered man's proper and necessary attitude were "repent" and "believe"; the one is man looking at his sin, the other at his Saviour. Repent was the first word used in Christ's preaching, and it never disappeared from his thought; it must then have meant to him a great truth. He preached it as a fundamental necessity: God's rule in men's hearts could not take place without their repentance. Christ said he came to call sinners, and Luke says in explanation he came to call them to repentance. Jesus said it would be more tolerable for Sodom and Gomorrah, though notoriously wicked, than for the generation that does not repent. He linked it with heaven's joy by saying "there is joy in the presence of the angels of God over one sinner that repents." Christ's aim was to establish the kingdom; he continually aimed at getting men into that kingdom, and the first condition of entrance was "repent."

2. *The need and meaning of repentance.* The need is based on the great truth that sin is ugly and holiness is beautiful; when a man comes to see that he will change his mind and forsake sin, and this is the meaning of repentance: a change of mind about it, a change of attitude toward it. Repentance has primarily nothing to do with sorrow or crying or emotion; some experiences with sin may lead to these and so help to bring about one's change of mind, but the repentance itself is simply changing one's mind toward the evil. To a man who is seeking his own interests Jesus says, "Change your mind, seek the kingdom"; to a life that is living for the pleasure of a sin, enthralled in its fascination and hungering for its next indulgence, Jesus says, "Change your mind, don't think of sin in its fascination but see its danger and its heinousness"; to a life that is indifferent to its highest ideals and making its own selfish interests its controlling motive, Jesus says, "Change your mind about it, and see that instead of being secondary your spiritual life is foremost and should be most carefully cared for." It is Christ's call to share in his view of sin and to break off from it, to stand with changed mind—ready for a better way. Repentance may be accompanied by sharp pain, or it may be calm and quiet; the pain is not the repentance and may not be there. The pain of repentance can only accompany the consciousness of sin, and the consciousness of sin can only be in proportion to the experience of sin. If one has had a horrible experience with the vileness and the dirtiness and the foulness of sin, then the pain, with bitterness and tears, are to be expected. But if one has not thus been baptized in sin he need not expect to be baptized in tears before he can repent. It should also be remembered that repentance is not a single and final act; we have the privilege of repenting at any commission of wrong. To do wrong with the deliberate intention of afterward repenting is not

worthy the name repentance; it would be only another phase of "indulgence." But when one yields to temptation and falls the chance to rise again is there. Indeed, repentance should be a continuous mental state, a continuous sharing with Christ his estimate of sin ever leading us to break with individual sins, and continuously aiming to forsake the lower for the higher ways of living.

3. *Our attitude toward Christ is expressed by the word faith.* Our attitude toward sin is expressed by repentance—looking back at it and forsaking it. The next step is to look forward: this is done in faith. In this two mental acts take place: (1) We accept the testimony that Jesus has come into the world to save sinners. The man who doesn't know this historic fact cannot of course exercise any faith in him; he cannot think of him in any way. The man who has the Bible and knows the facts of the life of Jesus comes to believe that they are true, just as he believes any other well-attested fact of history. (2) Persuaded of the truth of Christ we then become willing to commit ourselves to him to do for us what he claims he will do. Just as sinning is a deliberate choice of the will so faith is a deliberate act of the will: it is the expression of our attitude toward him as the Saviour and Lord of our lives. It is trusting, following, relying on Christ. The fact of God's love and willingness to forgive is presented: we accept the fact and act on it, just as we accept the fact of money in the bank and draw checks on it.

4. *Faith is not all passive but carries with it some endeavor.* Faith is not simply the opening of our hands to receive what Christ has done for us, it is also the use of our hands in doing something for him. It is not merely receptivity but use of what God bestows; it is an attitude to receive from the divine and also to be in sympathy with the divine. When we believe in God and commit ourselves to him we mean that we will actively endeavor to become

and do like God. Faith is the condition of deliverance from sin because it is man's expression of his desire to be delivered, and of his conviction that God is willing and able to deliver. To have that attitude and not follow it up with moral endeavor would be like having the sun without the sunbeam. Faith is man's right attitude toward God; it introduces man into right relation with God, because it is accepting God's forgiveness, and placing one's self in the attitude of obedience. God accepts a man on that faith as truly as we accept him on faith; we believe it is his intention to be kind and forgiving and helpful; God accepts our faith as our intention to do right. He takes the will for the deed if we are unable to perform the deed.

5. *It should be emphasized that faith is not the ground of our acceptance but only the condition.* When a man seeks acceptance with God and comes desiring to be saved, he can present no adequate righteousness of his own; the best he can do is to show a disposition to be and to do right. God cannot accept a man and seek to help him to be good unless he wants to be; that desire or disposition on man's part is expressed in faith—believing Christ and committing himself to him. But the faith has no merit in itself; the reason why God forgives and saves is because of his infinite grace, because he loves a man so that if the man will only let him he is more than willing to accept him. Yet God must know that he is willing; he cannot save—forgive and help in the making of a character—without a man's consent and desire: faith is the expression of that consent and desire. God must have this, though in the nature of the case, it betokens no desert on man's part: God forgives a man not because he deserves it, but because he treats a man better than he deserves.

6. *Two things need to be remembered:* (1) Faith and knowledge are not identical. Some people will say: "I can't accept all the things some persons do; I can't believe

them." It isn't necessary that they should in order to have faith. We should be careful to distinguish between articles of belief and faith, between the contents of our creed and reliance upon God. We do not have to understand all about God in order to have faith in God. We may know very little and yet have faith; perception of truth is one thing, willingness to accept truth is quite another. One's faith is governed more by his will than his intellect. Explanations about God and salvation do not bring men to accept them. Faith is not knowledge of God but capacity for God. In faith the soul goes out to an unseen reality; it is relying upon spiritual things that cannot be proven and that need not be proven; it is confidence in a loving Father who cannot be seen but is felt in every human breast to be real. (2) We may begin the Christian life with a very small faith. We may have full knowledge or small knowledge and faith be very weak. The life that goes out to God in trembling faith, through the most distracting of doubts, can be sure of finding a place in God's heart. Faith is not dropped down from heaven by magic or developed in a moment, it must be "wrought out of our own moral and spiritual experiences." We are simply to act on what we do believe; faith as small as a mustard seed will grow provided we plant it. We can increase our faith by working for it; people who have great faith have been people of great effort after faith. The difference in people's faith is not in the cast of their minds or the make-up of their dispositions, but in the schooling they have chosen to give themselves. If one man's faith is greater than another's it is because one has sent his faith to school while the other has allowed his to play truant. A man may begin with groping faith and faltering trust, but if he will educate his faith, make an anvil of his doubts, take his experiences not as temptations to doubt but as occasions for trust, he will soon find that he will come to know God with the certainty of his own breath, and come into a strengthening possession of the Divine Presence.

Topics for Class Discussion

1. The meaning of repentance.
2. Why faith is necessary to deliverance.
3. The relation of repentance and faith.
4. The active side of faith.
5. The relation of faith to knowledge.

Topics for Class Papers

1. Faith the condition, not the ground, of our acceptance with God.
2. The growth of faith in the Christian's experience.

LESSON V

THE KINGDOM OF GOD

W. H. Geistweit, D. D.

Reference literature. Bruce, " The Kingdom of God "; Boardman, " Kingdom "; Stevens, " The Teaching of Jesus," Chap. V; Vos, " The Teaching of Jesus Concerning the Kingdom of God and the Church "; Schwab, " The Kingdom of God."

1. *Jesus and the coming kingdom.* We cannot do effective work in teaching others unless we have clear conceptions of the fundamentals of the gospel. Jesus came declaring the kingdom of God at hand. All through his life he held prominently before his disciples the fact of a new kingdom which he had come in an especial sense to establish. God was among his people through all the ages. He never left the world without some witness of himself. But Jesus Christ came in the fulness of time to reveal the mind of God as was not possible before his day.

2. *What is the kingdom of God?* What is meant by the kingdom of God as Jesus used the term? It may be well to say that the terms " kingdom of God " and " kingdom of heaven " are here considered as meaning the same thing. There have been fine differences drawn between the two terms, but the writer contends that Jesus used them interchangeably. It seems to be fanciful hairsplitting to draw a distinction between them. Let us get the matter clearly before us. The kingdom of God is not a place established somewhere in the earth. Now and then there are some earnest and sincere people who seek to establish religious communities in which none but believers are admitted. But

religious communities are not the kingdom of God. Sometimes organizations are created with a view of realizing the kingdom of God, but the kingdom of God is not in organization. It is not determined either by geography, institution, or constitution. So the "church" is not the kingdom of God. It may be, and often is, the best expression of the principles of the kingdom of God, but the church is not the kingdom. Nor is it a "social State." The State may be purified, the citizens made comfortable, poverty abolished, equality extended to all men; but the kingdom is not necessarily created by these things. They may be expressions of some great principles of the kingdom, but they are not the kingdom. If we keep these things in mind, much confusion might be avoided in our discussions of the relation of the "church" to the world. The church by its institutions can bring men to a consideration of the character and claims of the kingdom of God, but the church cannot create the kingdom of God for men. Changing the circumstances of life does not necessarily change the real character of life. For circumstances may not affect the heart of a man. Place never makes the citizen, nor can it unmake him.

A sensible working definition of the kingdom of God ought to be comparatively easy for us. There is no need of difficult processes of reasoning where the Bible has such sunlight teaching. It is true that spiritual things are only spiritually discerned, but every one ought to be able to comprehend what Jesus meant when he came declaring the kingdom of God. Beginning with the teaching of John the Baptist the doors were opened to all men in a very peculiar way. All sorts of people came to hear the preaching of John. Without regard to nationality or religious condition he declared the same teaching to all. There was but one gospel, there was but one way to realize the new teaching. Jesus came declaring the same gospel, in clearer light it is true, but essentially the same gospel. He was continually battling against the wrong ideas and ideals of the Jews. They had a notion of the kingdom; it meant the re-establishment of the Jew upon the throne, the overthrow of the Roman, the general subduing of all the enemies of Israel, and an earthly glory imparted to the old people of God. But had Jesus accomplished all these things he would not have restored to them the kingdom of God, or ushered them into it. He might have helped their social condition, but they would not have been brought even to the entrance of the kingdom of God—as he declared it.

Coming to the more positive aspect of the theme, we ought to be able to clearly comprehend the teaching on this subject. To make a mistake is to create a calamity. The kingdom of God is a new life, created of God in the human heart. It is a spiritual movement in the soul by the Holy Spirit. It is a change of citizenship, of soul citizenship. *It is a new life.* It is a condition of heart, which establishes one in the great things of the gospel. "The kingdom of God is not meat and drink; but righteousness, and peace, and joy in the Holy Ghost" (Rom. 14 : 17). Here the meaning is so clear that the simplest mind can take it in. Place has nothing to do with it, nor position, nor things—the kingdom of God is an inner possession; it is the gracious work of the indwelling Spirit.

3. *Citizenship in the kingdom.* If this is so, the question of citizenship in the kingdom becomes simple. No man has a monopoly of spiritual things. Every human being may enter the kingdom of God. It is open to all men. The citizenship becomes a heavenly citizenship. Though one lives on the earth, he has rights and titles to other possessions of which the world knows nothing. He may have a stone for a pillow, a wilderness for a home, he is yet a child of God, an heir of the kingdom of our Lord and his

Christ. Such is the democracy of the kingdom of God—there is no respect of persons. Possibly the story of Nicodemus in the third chapter of John furnishes a good working basis for a full answer to the question of entrance to the kingdom. Nicodemus is a religious man—evidently not in the kingdom of God. Jesus says to him that the way into the kingdom is by being born again. There must be a movement of God upon the human soul before one can even see the kingdom of God. How little do men understand the kingdom in the light of this utterance of Jesus. Unless a man is born from above he cannot even see the kingdom of God. So the entrance to the kingdom is a spiritual entrance; we come into it by way of the work of the Spirit upon our hearts. Joining the church, therefore, is not entering the kingdom; submitting to a rite, or ceremony, or "sacrament," is not entering the kingdom of God. We are born into the kingdom just as we are born into the world—save that the entrance to the kingdom is a spiritual transformation of the inner life. Though men may not always see it, the citizen of the kingdom ought to be conscious of it beyond a doubt. "As many as received him, to them gave he power to become the sons of God, even to them that believe on his name: which were born not of blood, nor of the will of the flesh, nor of the will of man, but of God" (John 1 : 12, 13). Entrance to the kingdom of God is by way of receiving Jesus. Ours is simply the responsibility of receiving, believing Jesus.

4. *The work of the kingdom.* The work of the kingdom of God in the earth is purely on individual lines, though the individual so united to the kingdom ever unites himself with other members of the kingdom. He cannot go alone. The New Testament knows nothing of one member of the kingdom refusing fellowship with other members of the kingdom. It should result in the spiritual unity of the members of the kingdom of God. Here is the

natural use of a church; it becomes the expression, the organized expression of the kingdom of God. There is nothing like it in all the world. While the church is not the kingdom of God the church should be part of the kingdom, the sensible and true expression of the eternal principles of the kingdom which shall never pass away.

5. *The outlook of the kingdom.* The kingdom of God has a great outlook. It contents itself with nothing short of the complete winning of the world to Christ. True, its principles are sometimes turned aside, and men in their greed and selfishness ally themselves with the kingdom of darkness. But the leaven of the kingdom is working, and the effect is spreading throughout the world. There are many instances of its effect in these days. The growth of the peace idea, the desire to stop war, the growing willingness to arbitrate differences—these indicate the growing power of the kingdom of God. The work of amelioration, helping the poor, caring for the sick, hospitals, infirmaries, care for the children—these things indicate the growing influence of the kingdom of God in the earth. Such humanitarian works were unknown before Christ came declaring that the kingdom of God was at hand. In the beginning the work seemed small, but great things greet our eyes as we look about us. No, not all men who engage in these things are in the kingdom, but they are not far from it; so close are they that the principles of the kingdom affect their lives, even though they are unconscious of, or do not seem to care about the Master who came declaring the kingdom of God. The Christian's attitude should be in the spirit of the prayer which Christ taught his disciples: "Thy kingdom come." It should be our aim to extend the kingdom throughout the whole world. The kingdom of God is ever coming in increasing power, and we should hasten its complete triumph. The day is coming when the "kingdoms of the world are to

become the kingdom of our Lord, and of his Christ" (Rev. 11 : 15).

Such is the simple teaching of the Book upon the great theme of the kingdom of God. Where there is a man who has accepted Christ, no matter what his race, condition, place, he is in the kingdom of God. Thenceforward should he seek to tell men of the great and glorious kingdom of our Lord. He should seek by life, by influence, by service, to give the knowledge of the glory of God to all men throughout the whole earth. Here is the gracious fact of personal citizenship; here also is the great missionary plea to go to the ends of the earth and preach the gospel to every creature.

Topics for Class Discussion

1. What is the kingdom of God?
2. The kingdom of God in the Old Testament.
3. Jesus' relation to the coming kingdom.
4. The relation of the kingdom to the church.
5. The outlook of the kingdom of God.

Topics for Class Papers

1. The nature and the work of the kingdom.
2. The citizen of the kingdom of God and his earthly relations.

LESSON VI

THE CHURCH AS THE WORKING INSTITUTION OF THE KINGDOM

Reference literature. Dargan, "Ecclesiology"; Marsh, "The New Testament Church"; Harvey, "The Church"; Dargan, "Society, Kingdom, and Church"; Mathews, "The Church and the Changing Order."

1. *What is the church?* The word translated church in the New Testament is from a Greek word, meaning a called-out assembly. Its ordinary use in the New Testament is to designate a specific local assembly of Christians, organized for the worship of God and spread of the gospel. It was thus a congregation of believers in Christ—these believers having made an open confession in baptism that through their faith in Christ they had passed from death unto life. Each church was therefore a spiritual assembly. So far as the New Testament is concerned, the word church is never used as a designation of a universal visible church, or of a national or denominational church. It seems safe to say, however, that the word church is used sometimes in the New Testament in a generic sense. "In 1 Cor. 12 : 28, where Paul says: 'God hath set some in the church, first apostles, second the prophets,' etc., the local sense is still possible, meaning any local church, and so all the local churches. But the mention of the apostles, who were not over the local churches, but over the whole body of Christians makes it possible that even a more general sense of the word is here intended. A very interesting passage is 1 Tim. 3 : 15 where Paul says: 'The church of the living God, the pillar and ground of the truth.' Here the generic sense is more clearly apparent. It is

impossible to restrict the meaning here to any local church, and yet the local coloring is so strong that the phrase can hardly be considered to mean the whole general body of Christians, or the church universal in its broadest sweep. These latter two are of course possible meanings. It may be the general body of Christians visible on earth, or the whole church universal in all times and ages, and many interpreters adopt this view, but there seems to be in the apostle's use here a general sense of the local church to which we have analogy in many familiar expressions. For example, we say, 'The family is the social unit, the school is the hope of the country.' Here we do not mean any particular family or any particular school, and certainly there is no universal sense in which such language could be employed. We mean the institution, 'the family,' 'the school' used in what might be described as both a particular and a general sense at the same time." (Dargan.) "The church as an institution is somewhat difficult of definition. We have a great number of churches, from the vast organization of Rome to the group of men and women in some little town who are attempting to reproduce the democracy of primitive Christianity, but it has been argued that the church in a generic sense does not exist. But such precision is hardly justified by the ordinary usage of the terms. When we speak of the church we mean institutionalized Christianity, the Christian religion as represented by its organized adherents." (Mathews.) Thus when we speak of the church as the working institution of the kingdom we mean both the local church and the generic church as containing the organized forces for the spread of the kingdom of God.

2. *The relation of the church to the kingdom.* In the previous lesson it was said: "The work of the kingdom of God in the earth is purely on individual lines though the individual so united to the kingdom ever unites himself

with other members of the kingdom. He cannot go alone. The New Testament knows nothing of one member of the kingdom refusing fellowship with other members of the kingdom. Here is the natural use of a church; it becomes the expression, the organized expression of the kingdom of God." The kingdom of God thus includes the church as its most important working force. "The church is the visible earthly form of the kingdom and is the divine organization appointed for its advancement and triumph. Organized and governed by the laws of the invisible King, and composed of the subjects of the heavenly kingdom, who by the symbol of baptism have publicly professed allegiance to him, the church fitly represents that kingdom. Hence the apostles, in receiving authority to establish under divine inspiration the form and order of the church, received 'the keys of the kingdom of heaven.' Wherever they gathered disciples they organized a church; and at their death they left this as the distinctive and only visible form of the kingdom of Christ on earth. Thus divinely constituted and inspired, the church is God's organization, in which the Holy Spirit dwells, and from which divine spiritual forces go forth to transform the world from sin to holiness, and subject it to the sway of Christ." (Harvey.)

3. *The organization of the church for service.* The organization of the New Testament church is very simple and very democratic. Every member was to have a part in its conduct and work; it was thus congregational in form. All ecclesiastical power was exercised by each local church assembled as a congregation; and the decisions thus made in the individual church were subject to no reversal by any other ecclesiastical body. The power of receiving, disciplining, excluding members was inherent in each church. So too the power of electing its own officers and appointing its various members to some specific service. Paul, when addressing the church, ordinarily speaks of

the church as organized with bishops and deacons, the word bishop meaning the same as our word pastor. Each of these officers had his special work. They were leaders and not rulers of the church; nor did they exercise any priestly functions, for in the church each member was his own priest under God. These officers belonged to the local church only. Besides these Paul speaks of other officers, as follows: "When he ascended on high, he gave some apostles, and some prophets, and some evangelists, and some pastors and teachers, for the perfecting of the saints, for the work of the ministry, for the edifying of the body of Christ" (Eph. 4 : 8-13). These officers, with the exceptions of "pastors" and perhaps "teachers," seemed to belong to the generic church. Their labors were devoted chiefly to the building up of Christianity in general through the organization and up-building of local churches. In the earliest times there was no general organization of the churches, such as associations and conventions, for work, though it is more than likely that these soon came into existence—how soon we know not. They were the logical outgrowth of the missionary impulse of the church. So far as these associations, conventions, and so forth, do not mar the simple democracy and independence of the churches, they are surely in keeping with the divine will. Further, institutions of the church in the generic sense, created by the common spirit of Christianity are likewise to be recognized as expressions of the providence of God in the church. Most of the organized forces for religion to-day are the outgrowth of the church, either as a local body, or as institutionalized Christianity.

4. *What is the work of the church?* The sphere of the church's work is found in society. There have been many schemes for the improvement of human society, but we have seen that the divine plan is found in the kingdom of God, and that the church is the working institution of that

kingdom. The work of the church may be summed up under four heads: Evangelization, education, benevolence, and moral reforms.

(1) The first work of the church is evangelization. This is simply giving the gospel of Christ to mankind. It is the preaching of the "good news" to every creature. The fundamental need of this is seen in two facts: first, the sinfulness of man and his hunger for deliverance from sin; and second, the gospel of Christ is the only means of bringing this deliverance to him. Men must be brought to repentance for sin and to a saving faith in Jesus Christ the Saviour from sin, and this is to be done by what Paul calls "the foolishness of preaching." In the prosecution of the work of evangelization, the church must ever keep in mind the spiritual needs of mankind, but it must also point out the social significance of the gospel. The evangelism that fails to take into consideration the social needs and relations of man is doomed to failure to-day.

(2) The church has always been more or less interested in education. Indeed, part of preaching is distinctively educational. In a very true sense a large part of religious education is evangelistic. It teaches the truths of God to the child or the man with a view to winning the response of the soul of each to God. Instruction is therefore a very important part of true evangelism. The strongest ministry has therefore always been a teaching ministry. One of the most hopeful signs of the greater progress of religion to-day is the constantly increasing emphasis upon the need of religious education, and for a teaching ministry in the church. The Sunday-school, which is the church at work in teaching the message of God, is the greatest evangelistic field of the church to-day. It must be remembered that evangelism here is to be educational—teaching the truths first, and then appealing to the soul to respond to the message which these truths bring. Further, religious

education is concerned with teaching those who have been won to Christ to observe all things whatsoever he has commanded. The church must thus provide the way for the study of the great truths of Christianity, and their bearing upon the living of the Christian life in the midst of time, and the hope of that life for eternity. Religious education thus includes a study of both the ethics and the doctrines of Christianity. Just as we know the truth as it is in Jesus we become free in our moral and religious thought and life. More largely the church is concerned also with education in general. "The Christian church from the very first centuries naturally connected itself with the school." It has been the creative force back of the progress in general education. Most of the great institutions of learning were founded by the church. We should see that it does not lose this great distinction in this age of science.

(3) The next great work of the church is along the lines of benevolence. From the first the Christian church was deeply interested in charities. The spirit of brotherhood led the church in Jerusalem in its early days to share all things in common with each other. Collections were constantly being taken for the poor saints at Jerusalem by the Gentile churches. This benevolence of the church enlarged with its progress among mankind, taking on many forms of expression and finding its culmination in the thousands of benevolent institutions in the world to-day. "In fact it is one of the chief glories of Christianity that in every age of its unfolding power among men it has reached out a helping hand to the help-needing classes of mankind." It has covered the globe with countless institutions of mercy, absolutely unknown to the whole pagan world. More than ever must the church be keenly alive to-day to its obligation to carry on and even extend this work of benevolence. The church cannot turn this

work over to social settlements and other independent organizations without being stigmatized as an unsocial institution.

(4) Last of all the church must take part in the moral reforms of which society ever stands in need. This is especially true in our age, with its many reformers and would-be reform movements. "The name of reform is legion; yet there are some leading varieties which by way of illustration may be here noted. There is a great temperance reform, the breaking up of the drink habit and the destruction of the traffic in intoxicating liquors. There is a great movement for social purity, the checking of vice, and the encouragement of a better sentiment in regard to chastity. Then there is the problem of the better distribution of wealth, an effort to remove in some way the grinding inequalities, the awful contrast between the too rich and the too poor. Another great movement is that for the moral improvement of the 'submerged tenth,' the cleaning out of the slums. Still another vista opens before us in the way of sanitation and hygiene, the protection of the health of the community. Nor must we fail to take account of political reforms, more especially municipal politics.

"How now are the churches concerned with these various efforts for the improvement of the moral and social conditions of our time? This is a perfectly natural and proper question, and our answer would be in the apostolic language, 'much every way, chiefly because to them are committed the oracles of God.' The Lord has concern for human good, and the churches represent him on earth; but they need to take the greatest care and to exercise the greatest wisdom in order that they may not misrepresent him." (Dargan.) The time is now here for the church to take back some of the work lost from its rightful service.

Topics for Class Discussion

1. What is the church?
2. The relation of the church to the kingdom.
3. The work of the church in the world.
4. What is the proper attitude of the church toward moral reform?
5. What is the weakness of the church to-day?

Topics for Class Papers

1. The church as a divine institution.
2. The church as the working institution of the kingdom.

LESSON VII

LOVE, THE LAW OF THE CHRISTIAN'S LIFE

Reference literature. Drummond, "The Greatest Thing in the World"; Hopkins, "Law of Love"; Smyth, "Christian Ethics"; Dawson, "The Empire of Love"; Simpson, "Love Never faileth"; Boardman, "Coronation of Love."

1. *The supreme ethical need is love.* The world is not suffering for more law but for more love. It has always been a cold-hearted kind of a place. Throughout the ages men have been dying because they felt that no one—not even God—cared for their souls. The greatest debt man owes to man is that of love. It is greatest because love is man's deepest need. Jesus saw this supreme yearning of the human heart after love and sympathy and came into the world to reveal to men God as the loving heavenly Father who cared for all men, even though they be wayward and sinning. In his view "God so loved the world that he gave his only begotten Son" to save men from sorrow and sin and death. Men knew God as power, as wisdom, and as law already. He came to show them God as love. He put his great throbbing heart down against the suffering heart of humanity and measured its deepest need. Knowing this need he went about to satisfy it. Bringing men into fellowship with God as a loving father he brought them to see that if all is law all is likewise love. The One who is back of all and in all and through all is a being of infinite love, and it is his will that men should live by the principle of love and thus satisfy the world's supreme ethical need.

2. *What is the meaning of Christian love?* The Bible

is largely a book of love, Jesus Christ is the revelation of God's eternal love, and Christianity is fundamentally a religion of love. But what then is the meaning of love in this Christian sense? It is not a sentimental feeling, or an emotional flush, though both may accompany it. Thayer says it means "to be full of good-will and exhibit the same." It is thus attitude and action. If Christian love is analyzed into its elements we shall find the following: First, it is the recognition of worth in man. It is seeing and appreciating the good that is in humanity whether that be little or much. Secondly, love is respect for and regard for the welfare of man. Christian love does not trespass upon the personality of any man by treating him with disrespect. Further, it stands four-square for the rights of every man, not violating those, and seeking to keep the sinful world from violating the same. Thirdly, love is once again the desire, deep and abiding, to share with humanity what we are and what we have, either in person or property. In Christianity no one liveth unto himself. To do so is to transgress the fundamental law of Christianity. Thus the Christian takes pleasure in the joys of his fellow-men, "rejoicing with those that rejoice"; he also sympathizes with them in their sufferings, "weeping with those that weep." The fourth and last element of Christian love is the desire to possess—to share in the lives and personalities of those we love. This has been termed the selfish element in love. In a sense this is true, but it is a perfectly proper element. Love is a social activity of the human soul. There can be love only where there is a reciprocating object of love. Even God desires to share in our lives. Christian love is therefore the recognition of worth in a person (even the meanest of men), respect and regard for the welfare of each and every man according to his place in the world, desire to share with men, especially those of the Christian family, what we have and what we are, and last, the desire to share in whatever of good we see in the persons with whom we have to do.

3. *The twofold expression of Christian love.* As we have seen, love is not simply a feeling or desire, it is desire in action. Hence Jesus calls for conduct consonant with the call of the spirit of love within. We are to love, not only in word but in deed and truth. "If a brother or sister be naked, and destitute of daily food, and one say unto them, Depart in peace, be ye warmed and filled, notwithstanding that he give to them not those things which are needful to the body," that is neither faith nor love. Love ever seeks to do and to give the "things needful." Of this love there is a twofold expression, on the one hand toward God, and on the other hand toward man. There are some to-day who would say with Abou Ben Adhem: "Write me as one who loves his fellow-men," apparently unmindful that God should be an object of their love as well as man. The biblical view, both from the Old Testament point and also from the New is for the twofold expression. In both the obligation is to love God with all the heart, mind, soul, and strength, and your neighbor as yourself. That is, we are to love God with all the power of our being, and our neighbor as much at least as we love ourselves. The truth is that the Christian, living in the kingdom of God, cannot help recognizing and responding to the claims of divine love. The reign of God in his heart, and the revelation of God in his spirit, ever call for adoring love. The blessed experiences day by day of living in fellowship with the infinite One create in him at times the feeling of the psalmist, "Whom have I in heaven but thee, and there is none upon earth that I desire beside thee." Thus we come to put God first in our love. But this does not lessen our love toward man. On the contrary it increases and strengthens it. The feeling of God's eternal love for man constrains us, as Paul says, to love

others. The truth is, we love men more the more we love God, for we see then that they are the children of our heavenly Father's care, even though they ofttimes be wandering children.

4. *Love the only basis of human brotherhood.* Men have dreamed of the brotherhood of man in many forms. Plato's, "Republic"; Sir Thomas Moore's, "Utopia"; and Bellamy's, "Looking Backward," are samples of this age-long dream. Again and again men have sought to convert these dreams into reality, but one by one the Utopian schemes have failed. There seems to be no solution to the problem of human brotherhood through these world dreams and schemes. They may be aids to it but that is all. It is plain from the vision of human need, and the insight into truth as Jesus saw them, that love is the only basis of brotherhood. He could preach the doctrine of the brotherhood of man because he offered a basis for it. Recognize the worthfulness of men, have respect and regard for the good you see in them, seek to share all that you have and are that is worth while with them, and open your heart to whatever they may have to give—then you will have the fact of brotherhood. God's love makes it possible for him to be fatherly to all men; so our love will make it possible for us to be brotherly to all men. The demand of Christianity, then, that we be brotherly as we move among men, is a just demand, because it offers us the basis of brotherliness in its fundamental law of life—love. This brotherhood of Jesus is not a stationary and mechanical form of organized life. It is a spiritual relation finding its proper expression in words and deeds according to the occasion of time and place and person. Thus it solves the ever-changing relations of men in a progressive civilization. We cannot establish brotherhood by making rules for our conduct, but by receiving and expressing the brother spirit of love. Rules are only for to-day. We

shall need new ones to-morrow, perhaps. "New occasions teach new duties." But the presence of love in our hearts will make us fulfil those duties as they come. More than this, love will divine the right duty or deed that I owe my brother at a given moment. It will make me see that I cannot lump human beings and treat them all alike, but that I must have respect to the personality and individuality of each. Furthermore, love will show us that we cannot deal with the same person in the same way every time—each time is a new time, and may need a new expression of our brotherhood. Let us preach brotherhood, but let us preach it upon this sure foundation of Christian love, and some day we shall find that the poor man loves the great, and the great man loves the poor, and the people living like brothers strife shall be no more.

5. *Christian love the unchanging and ultimate ethical law.* It is safe now to say that Christian love is the one unchanging and ultimate moral law for mankind. Certainly we are true to the Bible and its Christ when we say this. The Old Testament word is: "Hear, O Israel, the Lord thy God is one Lord; and thou shalt love the Lord thy God with all thy heart and with all thy soul and with all thy might and thy neighbor as thyself." Jesus accepted this word and confirmed it for the New Testament writers. Love is therefore the unchanging moral principle. All other laws are more or less local and temporary. Love is the one unfailing and eternal law. As Paul says, "Love never faileth: it beareth all things, believeth all things, hopeth all things, *endureth* all things." There is no place for love to cease for there is no place where it is not needed. As we have seen it is earth's supremest need, and heaven is full of it for God himself is love. Since love is the unchanging moral law, it is the ultimate law in the Christian religion, and is thus the greatest thing in the world. Jesus made it ultimate and greatest when he called

it his new commandment, and made it the supreme and unanswerable evidence to the world of the reality of his religion. Paul made it ultimate when he compared all other gifts as nothing to it, and said that of the three abiding Christian graces—faith, hope, love—"the greatest of these is love." Thus to him, love was the fulfilling of all law. Peter gave it the supreme place when he exhorted the Jews of the Dispersion: "Above all things have fervent love among yourselves." John gives us the climax on love as the fundamental principle of the Christian life when he says: "God is love, and he that dwelleth in love dwelleth in God, and God in him." To live a love-life then is to be godlike. Love is in deed and in truth the law of the Christian's life. "Beloved, let us love one another; for love is of God, and every one that loveth is born of God, and knoweth God. He that loveth not knoweth not God, for God is love" (1 John 4 : 7, 8).

Topics for Class Discussion

1. Why love is the world's supreme ethical need.
2. The meaning and expression of Christian love.
3. How Jesus revealed to us the love of God.
4. Love as a basis of true ethics.
5. How love leads to right moral actions.

Topics for Class Papers

1. Love as a basis for human brotherhood.
2. The empire of love.

LESSON VIII

THE LEADERSHIP OF THE SPIRIT IN THE CHRISTIAN LIFE

Rufus W. Weaver, TH. D.

Reference literature. Strong, "Systematic Theology"; Clarke, "Outline of Christian Theology"; Johnson, "The Holy Spirit, Then and Now"; Coe, "The Spiritual Life."

1. *What is the Christian life?* In the study of a converted person, one observes first a changed will expressing itself in nobler and more godlike life. Not only is the will changed but also the disposition. Holy love is awakened in the soul. The converted man knows that a radical change has taken place in his sub-consciousness. He possesses new interests, new relations, new affections, new incentives to holiness, new purposes, and new hopes. He is a new creation. In seeking an explanation for this transformation, he finds truth to have been the cause. The truth regarding the sinfulness of sin entered the arena of his mind and conquered, and he realized more vividly than ever before that he was a lost sinner. The realization of sin does not lead necessarily to a turning from sin. Yet it is a prerequisite of repentance. Knowledge of the truth is not then the ultimate cause of conversion. The realization of sinfulness was followed by a loathing of sin, a mighty desire to renounce sin that stirred his personality to its depths. A Power not himself was at work within him. The changed relation to sin was not the product of either his volition or the realization of a terrifying fact. The unseen worker was the Holy Spirit. The perception of the truth of the gospel was followed under the inspiration of the unseen Worker by a loving trust in Jesus

Christ as a personal Saviour. He then realized that his sins were forgiven and that he was a child of God. The successive states are variously described. The realization of sin is called the conviction of sin. The ministers of earlier days devoted much time in revival services to the preaching of sin. Their course was logical and wise. The turning from sin is called repentance. The turning to Christ in loving trust, is called faith. The two, repentance and faith, are considered as one; for there is but one action in turning from sin to Christ as the Saviour from sin. To this is given the name conversion. The process which no one can explain, that begins with repentance, if not earlier, and ends with the knowledge of sin forgiven, is called regeneration.

This spiritual change is variously described in figurative language as a new birth, a new creation, a begetting of God, a resurrection to walk in newness of life. These phrases describe the initiation of a new life of holy love, like the life of God. Life is the correspondence to environment—a continuous readjustment of internal relations to external relations. The Christian life has its environments and its readjustments. The Christian purpose is to realize in daily conduct a correspondence to the divine will. The Christian life is characterized by a new relation to God, a new kinship with God, and a new development leading to an increasing likeness to God.

(1) The new relation—justification. Righteousness and justification have in the Greek one root. To justify means literally to righten, to bring into right relations. Justification describes the new rightened relation that exists between God and the renewed soul. It is the sequence of regeneration. This relation has two aspects—the one objective, the other subjective. Viewed objectively, God affirms that the penitent believer sustains an acceptable relation to him. Viewed subjectively, the penitent believer

is conscious of being at peace with God. In regeneration, the emphasis falls upon the reality of the new life; in justification, the emphasis falls upon the reality of the new relation between God and the soul.

(2) The new kinship—adoption. The reconciliation of man to God through faith in Christ results in more than a mere reconciliation. This relation is described in Scripture as adoption. The word means literally "son-making." The universal Fatherhood of God is not taught in Scripture as many believe. Only believers realize the relation of children of God. To as many as receive Christ, to these is given "the right to become the sons of God." This relation explains the chastisement of believers—"God dealeth with you as sons."

(3) The new development—sanctification. The progress of the Christian life toward perfection is called sanctification. "It is to regeneration what growth is to birth." Sanctification is a progress toward perfection, not perfection attained. Into this process enter both human and divine elements. On the one hand the believer must work out his salvation with fear and trembling; on the other hand it is God the Spirit that worketh in him both to will and to do. The progress of the Christian life is toward the measure of the fulness of the stature of Christ. In all these relations and adjustments the Spirit is ever at work.

2. *What are the offices of the Spirit in the Christian life?* (1) In regeneration. The mission of the Spirit includes the convicting of sin, the emphasizing of the truthfulness of the gospel, and the affirming of the trustworthiness of Jesus as a personal Saviour. The Spirit awakens, woos, urges, and pleads with the soul. Through faith in Christ, the believer assumes an attitude of soul toward God, in which it is possible for the Holy Spirit to consummate the change of heart. In this experience the things that were

once loved are now hated, and the things which were once hated are now loved. A complete readjustment of the disposition, the appreciations, the affections takes place and the effects of this transformation appear in the field of consciousness and are manifested through the intellect, the feelings, and the will. The intellect recognizes God in Christ as the divine Lord and Saviour, the authoritative Teacher; the heart recognizes Christ as the object of supreme affection; the will, wholly surrendered, manifests its submission in loving obedience to Christ, and the supreme effort of the new Christian life is to reproduce, amid the changing circumstances of the individual life, Christ-like conduct. The soul, having received Christ, is born not of blood, nor of the will of the flesh, nor of the will of man, but of God. In this experience the soul is born anew through the Spirit.

(2) In justification. The renewing touch of the Spirit and the trustful surrender of the soul to Christ are the conditions of justification. From the human side, it may be said the believer is justified through faith, since faith is the stretching forth of the hand to receive the free offering of grace. From the divine side, justification follows regeneration, and from this viewpoint, the work of the Holy Spirit is not only the precursor but also the originating condition of justification.

(3) In adoption. The consciousness of divine sonship in the believer is due immediately to the Spirit. It is through the reception of the spirit of adoption "we cry, Abba, Father . . . and if children, then heirs, heirs of God, and joint-heirs with Christ." "As many as are led by the Spirit of God, these are the sons of God."

(4) In sanctification. Sanctification is the progress of the Christian life toward perfection under the leadership of the Spirit, and this progress is guaranteed through the divine reinforcement that the Spirit gives. The Spirit leads

in clarifying and impressing the truths that make for holy living. The Spirit reveals Christ more perfectly to the soul, and intensifies the soul's fellowship with him. The Spirit helps the believer in his weakness to pray acceptably and renews his spiritual life from day to day. The Spirit strengthens and beautifies the Christian virtues and deepens the soul's devotion to God. The Spirit evokes new faith in Christ and intensifies the believer's love for God, giving vividness to the consciousness of the indwelling God. These are but some of the first-fruits of the Spirit, but they give a sufficient guarantee that He who hath begun the good work shall perfect it unto the end.

3. *What are the limits of the leadership of the Spirit?* The leadership of the Spirit is the evidence that we are children of God. The leadership of the Spirit removes us from subjection to the law. The leadership of the Spirit produces the fruits of love, joy, peace, longsuffering, kindness, goodness, faithfulness, meekness, and self-control. In every Christian life receptive to the guidance of the Spirit the progress toward goodness is persistent and constant. Perfect goodness is evidently unattainable in this life. The rapidity of spiritual progress is measured by the completion of one's surrender to the Spirit's leadership. "No Christian has yet tested by experience how much the Spirit of grace can do." The early Christians possessed the consciousness of the Holy Spirit as a present force strengthening them in witnessing for Christ, imparting to them power to overcome temptation and to endure persecution gladly for Christ's sake. There is no good reason why the believers of to-day may not live under the guidance of the Spirit an equally triumphant life.

The New Testament and personal experience both affirm the guidance of the Spirit in daily life. There is danger, however, especially among men of shallow minds, of attributing to the Spirit effects due to personal caprice.

"Prove the spirits; for many false prophets have gone out into the world." The test given by John is loyalty to Christ; a further test is conformity to the teaching of the word of God.

The believer may quench the Spirit, grieve the Spirit. For regeneration does not destroy human freedom, and the believer may choose his own leadership rather than that of the Spirit. Impotent Christian lives furnish convincing evidence that the Spirit is limited in effectiveness by the unwillingness of Christians to submit to his leadership, and just so far the individual believer determines the limits of the Spirit's leadership.

Though the individual may quench the fires of enthusiasm that the Spirit kindles, and may limit within his own experience the power of the Spirit, yet abundant time remains for the successful consummation of the divine work begun. Final failure is metaphysically possible since the individual is free, but morally it is impossible, since God cannot fail in that which he has undertaken to do. The progress of the Christian life is not limited to this world. There is a world of larger activities, where the imperfect shall disappear in the perfect, the human shall realize the divine, and in that world where righteousness reigns the Spirit's perfect work shall be made complete.

Topics for Class Discussion

1. The personality of the Holy Spirit.
2. The spiritual life.
3. Regeneration in the light of psychology.
4. Sanctification.
5. Co-operating with the Holy Spirit in the winning of souls.

Topics for Class Papers

1. The use of the truth and the work of the Spirit in conversion.
2. Sanctification through the Spirit.

LESSON IX

JESUS THE SUPREME AUTHORITY IN RELIGION

Reference literature. Sabatier, " Religions of Authority "; Eaches, " Doctrines and Ordinances of the New Testament "; Angus, " Christ Our Life "; Meyer, " Glorious Lord "; Clarke, " Outline of Christian Theology," Part IV; Somerville, " St. Paul's Conception of Christ "; Moule, " Christ is All "; Gordon, " Ultimate Conceptions of the Faith."

1. *The need of authority in religion.* Religion has been variously defined. Schleiermacher calls it " a sense or feeling of infinite dependence." Menzies says it is " the worship of unseen powers from the sense of need." More fully defined religion is the response of the soul to an unseen though consciously felt power, in worship, in trust, and in obedience. Now it is plain from all these definitions that there is need of some ultimate reality in religion on which the soul can lean for support, and to which it can look for guidance. Just as in ethics which deals with the relation of man to man, we have an ultimate law—the law of love—by which all our moral acts must be tested, so in religion, we must have somewhere an ultimate authority to which we can bring all our religious feelings, hopes, and acts, to see whether they correspond to the real truth, or are simply visions of our own fancy and products of our physical condition. This authority must be a person in order to satisfy the deepest need of the soul. The soul of man is competent in religion to work out its problem of salvation and character only under the consciousness of God and his revelation as it is in Jesus the Christ.

2. *All religions have their authority.* It follows from what is said in the paragraph above that all religions set

up their own authority. Buddhism has its Buddha; the ethical religion of China has its Confucius; Mohammedanism has its Mohammed, and so forth. Christianity, the true religion, likewise has its ultimate authority. It has made many blunders in its search for this authority. Most of its efforts along this line have been dominated by ecclesiastical and theological notions rather than by biblical. As Sabatier says: "In the time of Ignatius infallibility (and authority) resided in the parochial bishop; in the time of Cyprian in the entire episcopal body; the Fathers of Basel and Constance found it in the council; they of the Vatican found it in the person of the pope. Protestants rejected all these authorities, and in the eighteenth century substituted for them the letter of Scripture, and even in certain places their confessions of faith." Our age is seeking as no other ever did to settle the problem of authority in religion. It is the livest question in religious thought to-day. It is the livest because when one form of authority seems undermined religion must find another. It is the nature of religion to set up some ultimate on which the soul may rest in peace. The answers to this question to-day among Protestants are many. Some say with Chillingworth, "The Bible and the Bible only"; some "The authority in Protestantism is the Bible accurately interpreted"; others say it is the words of Jesus; others yet, the religious experience within, or Christian consciousness; and lastly, a few make it composite and say, "the Bible, the church, and reason."

3. *Jesus the ultimate authority in religion.* It is time now to ask if there is a biblical, or better, a New Testament, answer to the question: What is the supreme authority in religion? Does Christianity in its earliest written records undertake to give an answer to the question? If this question is a vital question in religion, it would seem that the Bible would undertake to throw some light on it. It

would be well therefore for us to turn to its pages to see if such light can be found. We will not look long before we discover that the New Testament teaches plainly that Jesus the Christ is the ultimate authority in religion. He is not simply Saviour, Redeemer, Friend, but Lord and Master. The angels who announced his coming to the shepherds near Bethlehem said: "Unto you is born in the city of Bethlehem a Saviour who is Christ the Lord." John in his Gospel makes him not only the agency with God in creation, but the light and life of men, and this because he is "the light that lighteth every man that cometh into the world." The early church, as shown by the Acts of the Apostles, recognized and worshiped the risen Christ as the rightful Lord of their lives. Paul makes Jesus head over all things to the church, the one before whom every knee shall bow and every tongue shall confess. There are gleams of the Christ in the Old Testament. Moses spoke of that prophet whom the people would hear. Isaiah saw him as the Prince of Peace whose kingdom should be over all. But the sure word of all on this matter is that of Jesus himself. He claims supremacy for himself in matters of religion: "Ye call me Master and Lord; and ye say well, for so I am." "One is your master, even Christ." His parting words were "All authority is given unto me in heaven and in earth." Over the matter of Sabbath observance he claims to be Lord of the Sabbath. His teaching was with the assurance of authority—notice the oft-repeated "Verily, verily I say unto you." The people of his day recognized this authority, even when they rebelled against it. It follows from the New Testament point of view that Jesus is the supreme authority in religion. Not the Bible, but Jesus the Christ who created the Bible, not the church, but Jesus the founder of the church, is our ultimate authority in religion. Loyalty to Christ is therefore the order of the day for every child of God. This has been the Baptist position throughout all their days. It was the position of the early disciples and apostles.

Christian experience corroborates this teaching in the New Testament on the Lordship of Jesus. "It is certain Jesus sovereignly conquers hearts. When by whatever means, a word or an act of healing, men get a glimpse of the treasure of life which he bears in himself, the most simple or the most learned is joined to him in a bond of love and confidence which nothing can break. This influence of the person of Jesus continues to be exerted by the intermediary of his discourses, and especially of his death on the cross; he conquers us by his spirit and at once becomes our master, the freely elected master of our souls." This authority of Jesus over us arises from the revelation of his consciousness of God and truth, and of his indwelling fellowship with us through the Spirit. Hence, Jesus, as the historic Christ revealing the truth, and as the risen Lord sending the Spirit is the supreme authority. In finding the historic Christ the Scriptures are our guide.

4. *The nature and ground of Jesus' authority in religion.* We need not speak of this authority as absolute from the standpoint of the universe. Absoluteness belongs only to the infinite God and Father of all. According to Paul's thought, a time will come when Jesus will deliver up his kingdom to God that God may be all in all. But the authority of Jesus is ultimate for us who are living in the midst of time. It is ultimate because Jesus is the full and the final revelation of God to us. It is ultimate also because of the divine work which he carries on in the hearts of men, bringing them into fellowship with God. From this it is clear that the authority of Jesus is not in an institution he may have inspired, nor even of necessity in his words. His authority is personal. He himself is the truth, and his words have power only because they are the expression of

himself. The ground of Jesus' authority in religion is thus seen to be in his revelation of God, and in his impartation of the life more abundant. Now, since the revelation of God as the loving Father leads men to open their hearts for light and life from this Revealer, it follows that "the supremacy of Jesus among the religious teachers of mankind rests upon the verdict of life. One can predict the universal and final rejection of Christianity only as one shall forecast the universal and final denial of the will to live. Because the desire for life is deep and ineradicable, because it prevails more and more wherever existence is normal, Christianity is bound to become the religion of the world. The leader for an achieving humanity is He who came to give the life more abundant. No teacher so identifies his cause with life as Jesus does. As healer, as prophet, as personal influence, as man of faith and of works, his whole power is directed upon human society to turn it into a vast and vital joy. Wherever the instinct of life is imprisoned, there he is confessed as the supreme deliverer; wherever the desire for life prevails, there the Master of the Christian world is recognized as rightful king; and if humanity as a whole shall rise into the passion for the highest kind of life, we may be sure that humanity will choose as its Lord, Jesus Christ."

5. *The Christian's response to this authority of Jesus.* The world to-day seems restless under all authority. "For the last twenty years our universities have been opposed to authority, as such, in science. Everything has become an open question. We investigate not only atoms but the origin of morality, and the history of the idea of God. Our ethical teachers will not listen any longer to the appeal to statutory enactment as a basis for moral sanctions." This feeling is likewise everywhere present in religion. Many men have thrown off the authority of the church, the pope, and even the Bible. Some are turning away from Christ as

the proper authority in religion, and looking to the reason, or to Christian experience as the ultimate authority. This means only a partial response of the soul of man to Jesus, and this is the danger of the religious world to-day. It is thus fitting that every Sunday-school teacher should learn the true authority in religion, which is Jesus the Christ, and respond to him in complete loyalty and with the whole heart. Our attitude should be: "Where he leads I will follow," whether it be in the field of action or in the realm of thought.

This response is first to the historic Jesus and second to the risen Lord, who is in our experience by the Spirit. The historic Jesus is God's ultimate revelation to man; the historic teaching of Jesus is the final teaching in matters of religion. Response to the gospel of the historic Christ opens the way of response to the risen Christ. This experience of the risen Christ in the heart calls for ever deeper response. Christian experience is, therefore, a growing responsiveness to Christ. The process may be stated thus: "The evangelical history known in an imperfect manner, and understood not at all, perhaps misunderstood—that is the first step. Then there come, through the serious discipline of life, the new sympathy, the definite moral purpose, and the clarified vision. The evangelical history is studied anew with more attention, with profounder interest. Slowly the person of Jesus seems to come out of the mist, and to stand behind his words and works, and back of the whole series of events, with which his name is associated. The gospel is now a living symbol; and under it is the living Lord. Appreciation goes deeper and deeper into the soul, sees its content more widely and clearly, looks upon it with stronger assurance, and becomes conscious of it as acceptable and yet transcendent, as a possession and yet as the grand objective of all search, the unceasing inspiration of wisdom, and the final home of all authority and peace." Thus we come to have in part, the mind of Christ. Thus the authority of Jesus is completely established over us. Our knowledge of him in the Bible, and our experience of him in our hearts both teach us that our experience can never rise to the fulness of his consciousness of God and truth. Humbly and gladly, therefore, do we acknowledge him as the ultimate authority in religion.

6. *The authority of the Bible.* What now of the Bible as authority in religion? In Part I, Lesson IX, we saw that the existence of the Bible was due to Jesus the Christ. No Christ, no Bible. Further it was said above that the Christian's response to Jesus Christ as Lord in religion was first to the historic Christ as the full and final revelation of God to man in human history. This historic revelation of God in Christ we find in the holy Scriptures. "In the realm of spiritual truth," as Doctor Bitting says, "Christ is our only authoritative religious teacher; but the Bible, when fairly interpreted, is the supreme spiritual authority in matters of religious faith and practice." The Old Testament has authority because, as Jesus said, it testifies of him. The New Testament has authority first, because it contains the story of the person, work, and teaching of Jesus among men, and second, because it contains the Epistles of Paul, Peter, John, and other writings in which the way of salvation through Christ is interpreted and adapted to the needs of humanity by men who were inspired of God for this important work.

Topics for Class Discussion

1. Why man needs an authority in religion.
2. Man's effort to find this authority.
3. The biblical conception of the ultimate authority in religion.
4. The ground of Jesus' authority in religion.
5. The proper attitude of the Christian toward this authority.

Topics for Class Papers

1. The church as authority in religion.
2. The authority of the Bible in religion.

LESSON X

THE RESURRECTION AND ETERNAL LIFE

W. Woodbury Pratt, D. D.

Reference literature. Purves, "Life Everlasting"; Boardman, "The Epiphanies of Our Risen Lord"; Münsterberg, "Eternal Life"; Clarke, "Outline of Christian Theology," Part VI; Weir, "Human Destiny in the Light of Revelation"; Stevens, "Teaching of Jesus," Chap. IX, XV; Salmond, "The Christian Doctrine of Immortality."

1. *The world-hope of immortality.* Man is immortal. This conviction is as age-long and universal as the human race, and finds expression in the religion, language, and civilization of all nations. The ancient Egyptians evidenced their hope of immortality in their magnificent sepulchers, pyramid inscriptions, and belief in a future judgment for all men. The Babylonians and Assyrians believed in the Island of the Blest for the immortal man who escaped the deluge—an abode for heroes, where there was a "fountain of youth" and "a tree of life." The Chinese show their hope of immortality in ancestral worship. Among the ancients this belief in life after death was perhaps purest among the old Persians. As for Greece and Rome Pindar paints in glowing words the joys of Elysium, Homer hopes for happiness beyond for exeptional favorites, Socrates affirms that nothing evil can befall a good man after death, and that immortality was necessary to reward the good; Plato argues that the soul is immortal, Virgil teaches that the soul is the real man and at his death will escape its prison and breathe its native air in the Elysian realms, and Cicero says "there is in the mind of man a certain presentiment of immortality."

2. *The Bible doctrine of immortality.* The world-hope of life beyond the grave did not satisfy the longings of the human spirit. The ages waited for God to answer that universal longing by a clear revelation of life after death. To make the hope of immortality man's sure and permanent possession called for the Christ of God to come into the world and speak the message with authority; and in whom there would be manifest the power of an endless life. The Hebrew prophets were among the God-inspired men who saw in the star of hope the promise of eternal life and the resurrection of the body. "He shall swallow up death in victory, and wipe away all tears," says Isaiah. Through him God would ransom men from the power of the grave, and redeem them from death. Daniel plainly teaches not only immortal hope but gives the foregleams of the resurrection of the body. "Many of them that sleep in the dust of the earth shall awake." Doctor Edersheim says: "The hope of the resurrection-world appears in every religious utterance of Israel. It is the spring bud on the tree stripped by the long winter of disappointment and persecution." This faith shines out in the Hebrew poems again and again. "I will behold thy face in righteousness." "I shall be satisfied when I awake in thy likeness."

The Bible doctrine of man's endless being grows out of two primary roots: the nature of God and the nature of man. God is the living One omnipotent and eternal, gracious and just. Man God made in his own image and after his own likeness. He breathed into his nostrils the breath of live "and man became a living soul." Thus God breathed his own life into man. He planted the seeds of the eternal in man's moral constitution. "He hath set eternity in their heart." Hence "we are the offspring of God." In harmony with this man is called in the Greek New Testament *ho anthropos*, "the uplooker." The teachings of Jesus and the apostles confirm the teaching of the prophets, and demonstrate the great truth of the resurrection and eternal life, the resurrection of Jesus himself being the greatest of all proofs.

3. *The resurrection.* The resurrection of Christ is God's unanswerable proof that he was the Son of God, the Saviour of man. "I am the resurrection and the life; he that believeth on me shall never die." In these brave, bright words Jesus gave the gospel of the resurrection. And after he was crucified and buried the white-robed messengers from heaven witnessed beside his empty tomb, "He is risen." This is the easter message—"the gladdest note that sweeps the harp of faith." Jesus had said, "Because I live ye shall live also." The resurrection of Christ is the proof of that promise, and the foundation of the resurrection and eternal life of his people. This is Paul's message likewise to the Christians of Corinth, and it has passed into the creed of all Christians since that day—"I believe in the resurrection of the body." He shows how God will fashion anew this body of humiliation into the likeness of Christ's spiritual body. Of the powers of this resurrection body we knew little. This we do know, that it is "spiritual," deathless, heavenly, and like unto Christ's body in glory. Thus the resurrection body is not the natural body restored as in the case of Lazarus. It is a building not made with hands, eternal in the heavens. And for that body in heaven we groan in spirit, says Paul. This is the masterful aspiration of the Christian. Our only hope in realizing it is through Jesus the Christ who died and rose again.

4. *Eternal life.* The immortality of the soul, as we have seen, is fixed in the moral sense of the human race. But the resurrection and eternal life are truths peculiar to divine revelation, as found in the Bible. "Eternal life" and "everlasting life" do not mean the same in the Bible. Eternal life means more than continuance after death.

It expresses a quality of life which comes as a gift from God through faith in the Redeemer, and is in the possession of the Christian here and now. "He that believeth on the Son hath everlasting life." "God hath given to us eternal life, and this life is in his Son." "This is the life eternal that they might know thee the only true God, and Jesus Christ whom thou hast sent." This eternal life is a spiritual possession on this side of death, as well as after death. Divine judgment for sin is past for all who are in possession of this eternal life.

5. *Death and afterwards.* The Christian's departure out of this earthly sphere is not described by the word *thanatos,* or death. The death that is death means separation from fellowship with God. A man may be living in the world of art, or science, or commerce, and remain outside the kingdom of God. He who possesses the eternal life from God through Jesus is forever exempt from death in this sense. As Jesus says, "He is passed out of death into life." The dissolution of the body, which men call death, is a small item in the fact of death for the Christian. Sin, forever separating from God, is the great fact in real death—"The wages of sin is death, and the sting of death is sin." To the Christian the sting of death is plucked out. Hence Christ and apostolic writers substitute new terms to describe the passing of believers. Paul calls it "sleeping through Jesus." And this term does not mean the repose of unconsciousness, for there is no suspension of the spiritual life and activity for the Christian. Jesus in his death and resurrection abolished death, and brought life and the immortal body to light through the gospel. He came to deliver them who through fear of death were slaves. Hence Paul could speak of his departing to be with the Lord.

6. *What we know about the eternal life in the beyond.* Victor Hugo says: "I feel in myself the future life. I am rising I know toward the sky. The sunshine is over my

head. Heaven lights me with reflection of unknown worlds. Winter is on my head, and eternal spring is in my heart. The nearer I approach the end, the plainer I hear around me the immortal symphonies of the worlds which invite me." This is ever the Christian's outlook from the shores of time to those of eternity. Of this life beyond he knows only in part. "Eye hath not seen nor ear heard, neither have entered into the heart of man the things which God hath prepared for them that love him." But some things have been revealed unto us by his Spirit. First, we shall be like Christ. The spiritual body of believers shall be fashioned like unto Christ's body. If it doth not appear now what we shall be, we know, says John, "that when he shall appear we shall be like him, for we shall see him as he is." Secondly, we shall receive a suitable reward for the service we have rendered toward righteousness in the world of time. What these rewards shall be we may not know, but the promise is that not even a cup of cold water given in the name of a disciple shall be overlooked. Thirdly, our lives there will be in a realm of joy and peace. "God shall wipe away all tears from our eyes." We shall rest from our labors, which may mean that we shall enter upon other and nobler labors for the God who has redeemed us through Christ.

And only the Master shall praise us, and only the Master shall blame.
And no one shall work for money, and no one shall work for fame.
But each for the joy of working, each in a separate star,
Shall draw the thing as he sees it for the God of things as they are.

Fourthly, we shall know each other there. Paul says, "we shall know even as we are known." If we know each other here, surely it is perfectly reasonable that we shall know each other there. This opens up to us the joy of holy and loving fellowship in the endless ages of our eternal home.

Topics for Class Discussion

1. Job's question, the question of the ages.
2. Bible doctrine of immortality.
3. Jesus and the immortality of the Christian.
4. The nature of eternal life here and hereafter.
5. Shall we know each other in the life beyond?

Topics for Class Papers

1. The resurrection of Jesus.
2. He that hath the Son hath life.

9781333962074
SD - #0112 - 030225 - C0 - 229/152/9 - PB - 9781333962074 - Gloss Lamination